CLASS, CASTE, AND ENTREPRENEURSHIP

Class, Caste, and Entrepreneurship

A STUDY OF INDIAN INDUSTRIALISTS

E. Wayne Nafziger

ℛ *AN EAST-WEST CENTER BOOK*
FROM THE EAST-WEST TECHNOLOGY
AND DEVELOPMENT INSTITUTE

Published for the East-West Center
by The University Press of Hawaii
Honolulu

10-23-85

Copyright © 1978 by East-West Center

Manufactured in the United States of America

Library of Congress Cataloging in Publication Data

Nafziger, E   Wayne.
  Class, caste, and entrepreneurship.

  Bibliography: p.
  Includes index.
  1. Businessmen—India—Visakhapatnam.
2. Businessmen—India. 3. Entrepreneur—
Case studies. 4. Social mobility—India—
Visakhapatnam. 5. Social mobility—India.
I. Title.
HC438.V57N34   301.44'47'0954   78-16889
ISBN 0-8248-0575-5

Portions of chapter 3 previously appeared in "Indian Entrepreneurship: A Survey," in *Entrepreneurship and Economic Development* (© 1971 by The Free Press), edited by Peter Kilby (New York: The Free Press, 1971) and are reproduced here by permission of Macmillan Publishing Co. Portions of chapter 4 previously appeared in "Class, Caste and Community of South Indian Industrialists: An Examination of the Horatio Alger Model," *Journal of Development Studies* 11(2):131–148 and are reproduced here by permission.

To Elfrieda

CONTENTS

TABLES

ACKNOWLEDGMENTS

This work originated when I was Visiting Fulbright Professor at Andhra University under a grant from the United States Educational Foundation in India (U.S.E.F.I.). Most of the writing was completed while a Fellow at the Technology and Development Institute (T.D.I.), East-West Center. Additional financial aid was supplied by Andhra University and Kansas State University.

The field research was possible only with the support of Professor B. Sarveswara Rao, Head, Department of Economics, Andhra University, and the facilitation of W. Robert Holmes and C. S. Ramakrishnan from U.S.E.F.I. M. Jagadeswara Rao and S. A. R. Sastry assisted me in interviewing entrepreneurs, who spent hours answering questions. Officials from Visakhapatnam District gave considerable encouragement to the study.

The help of Hahn-Been Lee, Manuel Albe, and Louis Goodman, directors of T.D.I., and the criticisms of Richard Morse, Eugene Staley, Ben Finney, and Kanisetti Venkata Ramana improved the book substantially. Gary Hanson, John Richards, Alok Chakrabarti, Robert Buchele, Peter Kilby, Young-whan Hahn, Kusum Nair, G. Parthasaradhy, K. V. Sivayya, Paul Kelley, George Montgomery, Lelah Dushkin, William Richter, Krishna Akkina, and many others have also contributed to the study. Only Elfrieda, Brian, and Kevin could have cheerfully tolerated the disruption from travel between Nigeria, Andhra, Hawaii, Kansas, and England. I am deeply indebted to all who helped, but I am solely responsible for weaknesses.

1

INTRODUCTION

Perhaps one day a Saga may be written about the modern captain of industry. Perhaps, in the civilization which succeeds our own, a legend of the Entrepreneur will be thumbed by antiquarians, and told as a winter's tale by the firelight, as to-day our sages assemble fragments of priestly mythologies from the Nile, and as we tell to children of Jason's noble quest of the Golden Fleece. But what form such a legend may take it is not at all easy to foresee. Whether the business man be the Jason or the Æetes in the story depends on other secrets which those unloved sisters keep hid where they store their scissors and their thread. We have, indeed, the crude unwrought materials for such a legend to hand in plenty, but they are suitable, strange to say, for legends of two sharply different kinds. The Golden Fleece is there, right enough, as the background of the story. But the captain of industry may be cast in either of two *rôles:* as the noble, daring, high-souled adventurer, sailing in the teeth of storm and danger to wrest from barbarism a prize to enrich his countrymen; or else as the barbarous tyrant, guarding his treasure with cunning and laying snares to entrap Jason, who comes with the breath of a new civilization to challenge his power and possession.

Maurice Dobb, *Capitalist Enterprise and Social Progress,* p. 3.

Economists have been preoccupied with increasing the size of the economic pie while slighting its distribution. Despite the recent disenchantment with the viewpoint that all classes share in the benefits of industrial growth, empirical data on the distribution of income, business opportunity, and economic power are in short supply.[1]

Many studies on entrepreneurship and economic development either rationalize ruthless capitalist exploitation as Baran suggests[2] or glorify the capitalist entrepreneur without examining class origins and monopoly advantage. In his presidential address to the Economic History Association in 1946, Cole argues that "[t]o study the 'entrepreneur' is to study the central figure in modern economic history, and, to my way of thinking, the central figure in economics."[3] To Schumpeter, entrepreneurs, with varied class origins, and the dream and will to found a private kingdom, to conquer adversity, to achieve success for its own sake, and to experience the joy of creation are heroic figures.[4] In a scheme labeled a moral theory by one critic,[5] McClelland conceives the efforts of the entrepreneur, in his exercise of control over production in both capitalist and socialist economies, as largely responsible for the global association between a high need for achievement (a psychological measure of the urge to improve) and rapid economic growth. The entrepreneurial role is assumed to be characterized by moderate risk taking as a function of skill rather than chance, energetic and/or novel instrumental activity, individual responsibility, inner satisfaction that arises from having done well, an interest in money primarily as a measure of achievement, and long-range planning and organizational abilities.[6] For Papanek, the frugal, hard-working, far-sighted, remarkably able private entrepreneur willing to take political risks is in large part responsible for the "success" of Pakistan in achieving rapid industrialization.[7] Carroll has characterized Filipino entrepreneurs as exhibiting "a desire for independence; the drive, energy, and stamina which lead them to continue innovating and expanding even after their original goals have been achieved; a high level of intelligence; and the willingness to take calculated risks."[8]

Three recent empirical studies of the socioeconomic mobility of the entrepreneur have reinforced this heroic conception. Collins, Moore, and Unwalla found that most of the entrepreneurs in medium manufacturing firms in Michigan "clearly moved a long way from the somewhat impoverished economic level of their childhoods."[9] Both Nigerian and Greek industrialists were considered highly upwardly mobile in status by Harris and Alexander, respectively.[10] This view is consistent with the paradigm of neoclassical economics, which tends to disregard questions of class origin, to abstract from considerations of conflict and political power,[11] and to assume relatively open competition in a polity characterized by the balancing of independent interests.

The approach of this monograph is to consider the subject of entrepreneurship in a low-income country, not only for the objective of growth, but also for the goal of more equitable distribution of income, wealth, and economic opportunity. The discussion of some of the differences in entrepreneurial activity between castes, classes, and communities provides an insight into the extent to which official objectives, that the "backward classes" and "weaker sections" of the country share in India's economic growth, have been realized.

THE MAJOR QUESTIONS OF THE STUDY

Much of this study focuses on the origins of fifty-four manufacturing entrepreneurs in Visakhapatnam, a newly industrializing city in coastal Andhra Pradesh, India.[12] The study offers one perspective on vertical socioeconomic mobility, and the differences in economic opportunities between the privileged and underprivileged portions of the population. A highly disproportionate number of the industrialists (especially successful ones) are from twice-born castes and from families with a high economic status. Members of the dominant castes, leading classes, and large business houses can avert the threat of democratization and modernization to their families' positions by using the cumulative advantages of the past—property, influence, status, and so forth—to obtain the concessions, experience, education, training, and initial capital usually essential for successful entrepreneurial undertakings.

Even though I consider the literature on entrepreneurship narrow for neglecting the distribution of business opportunities within the population, I do not want to imply that considerations of economic growth and efficiency, and the development of entrepreneurial skills, are trivial. Economic growth (i.e., growth in output per person), despite its well-known costs, does increase the range of human choice. In the past, economists have attributed the sources of growth per head and increases in productivity per man primarily to the growth in the supply of physical capital. However, the accumulation of empirical evidence has recently undermined economic development theories based on the single factor of capital.[13] The result has been a shift in emphasis on the part of a few away from the growth of physical capital to the expansion of human skills, such as entrepreneurship, as the major determinant of the rate of economic growth. Thus, while some of the literature on entrepreneurship does not put enough emphasis upon social structure and economic stratification, in contrast to a large part of the economics literature, it at least has the virtue of placing man at the center of the drama to improve material levels of living.

Although I am not content to confine the questions only to the prevailing concerns of the literature, the scope of this study does include many of the same topics found in empirical studies of entrepreneurship in less-developed countries. Some of the empirical studies cited in chapters 2 and 3 have information on the education, training, occupational and socioeconomic background, social and religious community, sources of initial capital, and relationship to government of the entrepreneurs.

However, most of the works lack the data essential to the consideration of those factors related to entrepreneurial quantity and success. The determinants of the quantity of entrepreneurs may be found by comparing the data on the characteristics of entrepreneurs and the population as a whole. Indian census data are unusually rich, and provide information on migration, occupational backgound, education, literacy, and religion which can serve as a basis for comparisons between sample businessmen in Visakhapatnam and the population of the city as a whole. Also, I have utilized data from Ramana's scientific sample survey of Visakhapatnam, constructed from a sample frame based on a perusal of census records. Unlike the census, which has not gathered data on caste since 1931, the survey by Ramana has information on the caste composition of the city in 1970.[14] Thus, I am able to compare the caste composition of my sample with that of the population of the city as a whole—a comparison not possible in any of the other empirical studies of Indian entrepreneurship (see chapter 3).[15]

Factors related to entrepreneurial success are found by correlating caste, paternal economic status, education, work experience, sources and amounts of capital, and degree of government access of the entrepreneurs, to their income class and the gross value added of their firms (see Appendix A). Few other studies have access to these measures, which can be considered indicators of business success. Some economists would also consider these measures indicators of social contribution. The value added of an establishment measures its resource earnings, and thus, its contribution to gross national product. According to marginal productivity theory, under pure competition a person's income reflects what he is worth to the firm, and to society as a whole.[16] However, I make no claims that these measures bear a close relationship to social contribution. The assumption of pure competition is not warranted, as the evidence in chapter 6 concerning market imperfections, monopolistic restraints, barriers to the entry of new firms, and government support to inefficient enterprises indicates. Resource earnings are distorted by substantial variations between actual and equilibrium factor and commodity prices. A major distortion, discussed in chapter 6, is created by government controls and quotas. Furthermore, there are substantial divergences between the private and social cost and benefit of industrial production, which arise from such things as the development of human skills, and forward and backward linkages with other producers.

Clearly, where data are collected by interview, only a limited number of questions can be asked, since respondents have pressing duties, and a limited attention span. The cost of asking a question is the foregone opportunity of asking another question. My previous experience in interviewing industrial entrepreneurs in Nigeria,[17] together with my collaboration with colleagues in the Department of Economics at Andhra University, provided some guidance for the selection of questions.

Some of the factors considered in the selection of questions should be indicated. First, the faculty of the Department of Economics at Andhra University, Waltair, as part of their interest in providing advice for local government officials, had certain objectives. Although these were not a severe constraint, they resulted in a greater emphasis on an appraisal of government programs, and an omission of data on sources for expansion capital.

Second, the nature of findings and propositions from previous studies on entrepreneurship influenced the type of question asked. Questions pertaining to propositions well established in the literature, and unlikely to generate new information and new challenges, were usually omitted. However, questions were framed to test the consensus of the existing literature on important issues about which I had doubts and disagreements.

Third, certain interesting theoretical questions could not be asked without substantial cost in time and rapport with the entrepreneur, for instance, what kind of relationship do entrepreneurs and/or capitalists have with workers? In my previous experience, it was clear that respondents, when willing to answer at all, tended to be biased. Independent sources of information, available on other questions, are fewer. Competitors, suppliers, and customers in business, as representative of the capitalist class, are less likely to supply independent information on labor relations. On the other hand, interviews with workers would lessen the investigators' rapport with the entrepreneur and the amount of other information elicited, and change the whole nature of the field study.

Finally, my own professional background and research capabilities predisposed me toward certain questions, and precluded others, even though the study is multidisciplinary. Thus, although I evaluate the literature on achievement motivation and entrepreneurship in India from the standpoint of the social scientist (in chapter 3), I do not have the competence to test and score for need for achievement.

As a result of these factors, certain topics were not stressed in questions. Little emphasis was placed upon motivation or "inner driving forces" for becoming entrepreneurs.[18] Pretesting of the first draft of the interview schedule in ten firms indicated that in India, as in my previous sample in Nigeria, entrepreneurs either were puzzled that anyone would ask "why did you go into this business," or indicated a pecuniary motivation. One entrepreneur, in response to this inquiry, replied, "I can make more money doing this," and the expression on his face seemed to ask the question, "why else?"[19] In addition, the faulty and selective memory of the entrepreneur is less likely to distort impressions and misrepresent past occurrences when recalling employment, previous work experience, and sources of capital than when recounting motives, either in answer to an open-ended question or a choice of responses, which are usually neither comprehensive nor mutually exclusive. (See the discussion of Christopher's study in Appendix C.) It seems unlikely that an analyst, on the basis of a multiple-choice question concerning motives, can surmise that "more of the respondents were led to their [entrepreneurial] career by natural inclination to it than by anything else—that is, they felt an attraction to that career *in itself* apart from the attraction of profit prospects, the desire to follow father's business career, the pressure of urging by elders, the urge to contradict father, or the prestige expected in the career chosen."[20]

Rather than querying personal motivation, therefore, questions were directed toward acquiring data for analysis of the role of education, training, work experience, access to capital, caste, and paternal occupation and economic status in preparing the person for entry into industrial entrepreneurship (chapters 4 and 5). In general, questions requiring the entrepreneur to analyze his situation were not selected, in preference to those asking for his impression of facts. The respondent's own conception of the entrepreneurial role was not requested as has been the case in some studies of entrepreneurship.[21] The cost in further information lost in obtaining this is high and entrepreneurs have few insights to add to the existing literature.

SKETCH OF THE INDIAN ECONOMY

India has a population of 586 million (1974), second in the world only to the People's Republic of China, and an area (including Jammu and Kashmir) of 1,261,434 square miles, about equal to that of the United States east of the Mississippi River plus Minnesota, Iowa, Nebraska, Kansas, Missouri, Arkansas, and Louisiana. The area varies from tropical monsoon forest, tropical savanna, and tropical steppe in the southern peninsula to arid desert, semiarid steppe, and humid subtropical conditions in the northern subcontinental area (primarily north of the Tropic of Cancer), to moderate highlands in the Himalaya Mountain Ranges in Jammu and Kashmir, northern Punjab, Himachal Pradesh, and Uttar Pradesh. Population, growing at a rate of over 2 percent per annum, is increasing almost as rapidly as food consumption.

According to official data, India, with a gross national product (GNP) of $55.3 billion (or Rs. 414.6 billion) in 1972/73, had a GNP per capita of $97 (or Rs. 730), a real per capita rupee growth rate of only 0.8 percent per annum since 1960/61 (in 1960/61 prices). Real wage rates for factory workers have increased at an even slower rate. World Bank figures for 1970 rank India in the bottom fifth among countries in the world in gross national product per capita.[22] Despite the well-known inadequacies of international comparisons from national income data,[23] it is clear that the real level of material well-being is low, and its growth rate is not rapid compared to recent rates of less-developed countries as a whole.

In 1971, 60 percent of India's labor force was engaged in agriculture.[24] The percentage of gross product originating in the manufacturing sector, 13 percent, placed India somewhat below the median among countries in the world with data.[25] However, the proportion of gross product originating in the manufacturing sector has remained virtually unchanged since independence.

A BRIEF SOCIOECONOMIC SKETCH OF VISAKHAPATNAM

The setting for this study, Visakhapatnam (or Vizag), with a population of 355,045 (1971), is the second largest municipality in Andhra Pradesh, and the thirty-fourth largest urban agglomeration in India. The city is located on a major rail junction on the east-central coast of India (see fig. 1), about halfway between Calcutta and Madras. Vizag's port ranks next only to these cities and Bombay on the quantum of cargo handled.[26]

The physical appearance of Vizag suggests a series of contiguous towns or villages, many of which are residential enclaves with the population drawn from the same caste, ethnic community, or workplace. Visakhapatnam old town is a compact area of less than a square mile with a chaotic mix of land uses for commerce, services, government offices, and residences. The concentration of the major commercial activity of the city along the Main Road, about one mile long, with a macadam pavement about fifteen feet wide, chokes the movement of traffic during the peak hours. Since there are no proper footpaths for pedestrians or separation of fast moving vehicles from slower ones, the flow of traffic consists of the juxtaposition of buses, automobiles, lorries, jeeps, bicycles, rickshaws, oxcarts, handcarts, cattle, dogs, and pedestrians walking or carrying head loads.[27] Although disorderly land use and traffic patterns hamper efficiency, patterns in Vizag do not vary substantially from those in most other major cities, such as Calcutta.

Vizag's History

The town probably received its present name in the early years of the fourteenth century, when Kulottunga Chola of the Andhra dynasty encamped in the area, and built a temple dedicated to his favorite god, Visakha, the Hindu Mars.[28] Although the economy of coastal Andhra was primarily agrarian, from the eleventh century to the sixteenth century, towns and cities sprang up around the holy shrines and capitals of the kings of various dynasties. The demand which arose for textiles, oils, sugar, ornaments, metals, and furniture made the services of artisans indispensable and raised their ritual as well as economic status.

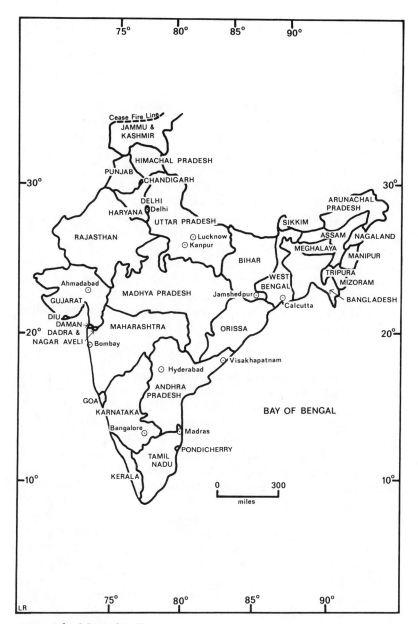

FIGURE 1. Map of India.

Beginning in the twelfth and thirteenth centuries, internal trade grew tremendously as (1) transportation and communication improved; (2) towns were created; (3) political stability increased, and (4) kings, chieftains, priests, and pilgrims became dependent upon goods sold by merchant communities.[29]

Although the Dutch became the first Europeans to settle in Vizag in the early seventeenth century, the settlement established by the English East India Company in 1682 constituted the foundation of the modern city. A primary stage in the urbanization of Vizag occurred, under British hegemony after 1802, when cultivators lost their customary rights to zamindars who were granted land ownership in perpetuity, and after Vizag became the capital of the district in 1803.[30]

The opening of the coastal railway in 1897 did provide some stimulus to the growth of Vizag. However, prior to the construction of a modern port between 1927 and 1933, Vizag was a small town with a population whose primary economic activities were fishing, petty trade, and household industry. Economic and population growth accelerated at a much faster rate after the development of the port and the building of a railway line through present-day Orissa and Madhya Pradesh in the 1930s.

The Vizag Economy

Four government or quasi-government establishments—the port trust, a ship-building yard, a naval base, and the railways—together with state and central government offices are the major employers in the city. According to the 1971 census, 71.5 percent of the working population living in the city is employed in services (including trade, commerce, transport, and communication), while 17.0 percent is in industry (i.e., manufacturing and household industry), 8.1 percent in construction, and 4.7 percent in agriculture, mining, and related activities. Industrial employment grew by over 200 percent between 1951 and 1961, and 73 percent between 1961 and 1971.[31]

Vizag serves as a port for exports from the vast hinterland of Andhra Pradesh, Madhya Pradesh, and Orissa, states rich in iron ore, steel, coal, and manganese ore. Most of the imports through Vizag port are crude petroleum, destined for the local refinery, and food, fertilizer, and machinery for distribution to the hinterland region.[32]

As a result of excellent harbor and railway facilities, the availability of both cheap unskilled labor and technically skilled manpower, a sizeable potential market, and the central government's encouraging attitude toward the location of manufacturing industries in "industrially backward" areas, there has been a post–World-War-II industrial boom in Vizag, especially in the last two decades. Major industrial enterprises in Vizag include Indian-U.S. ventures in oil refining and fertilizer manufacturing, and a central government undertaking in heavy plate and vessels, assisted by Czechoslovakian personnel. The ground-breaking ceremony for the construction of a government steel plant in the municipality took place in 1971, the same year in which entrepreneurs in the sample were interviewed. A number of smaller-scale manufacturing firms, some of whose entrepreneurs are the subject of this study, are ancillary producers (i.e., makers of components, subassemblies, or tools) for the larger-scale enterprises.

Population and Literacy

From 1921, just prior to the beginning of the construction of the port, to 1971, the population of the Vizag municipal area increased from 44,711 to 355,045 (a rate of increase of 4.23 percent per annum). The unprecedented urban sprawl in recent years, the result of substantial transport, commercial, and industrial development in Vizag, was accompanied by an extension of the city limits in 1966 (from 11.25 square miles to 29.47 square miles), and a population growth rate of 5.33 per annum between 1961 and 1971 (based on the extended area).

In Vizag, 48.7 percent of the population five years and older is illiterate (i.e., cannot read and write with understanding in any language). Among males 38.3 percent are illiterate, and among females 59.9 percent.[33]

2
PERSPECTIVES ON THE STUDY
OF ENTREPRENEURSHIP

THIS chapter provides a brief summary of the relevant literature on entrepreneurship and it is important as a background to the concepts and questions considered in the study. In the first two sections, I sketch the concept of the entrepreneur in the history of economic theory, and in contemporary economic analysis. In a subsequent portion of the chapter, I indicate why a particular concept of the entrepreneur is used in this study. The discussion of contemporary empirical studies on entrepreneurship in less-developed economies which follows is short, because of the availability of two excellent surveys on the topic. My purpose in this discussion is to emphasize aspects of the works that introduce issues dealt with in this study. In the last section prior to the summary, I indicate the major differences between this study and field studies by other authors.[1]

THE ENTREPRENEUR IN THE HISTORY OF ECONOMIC ANALYSIS
Early French Political Economists—The Development of the Concept of the Entrepreneur

The treatise of the French writer, Richard Cantillon, frequently considered the earliest systematic work in political economy, was probably the first to discuss the entrepreneur. Cantillon divided the inhabitants of a country, except for princes and landlords, into two classes: (1) entrepreneurs, including farmers and merchants, and (2) hired people. He distinguishes between the owner and the entrepreneur, although the two categories are not clearly spelled out. Entrepreneurs carry on the production and exchange of goods at some risk, facing the possibility of bankruptcy when the demand for their products is depressed.[2]

J. B. Say was probably the first economist to differentiate the function and remuneration of the entrepreneur from that of the capitalist. The entrepreneur directs acquired knowledge to the production of a good for human consumption. To be successful, Say maintains, the entrepreneur must be able to estimate future demand, determine the appropriate quantity and timing of inputs, judge and calculate probable production costs and selling prices, and supervise and administer. Since the combination of these is not common, the quantity of successful entrepreneurs is limited, especially in industry.[3]

The English Classical Economists—The Merging of the Entrepreneurial and Capitalist Functions

Although capitalism (i.e., the separation of the worker from the ownership of the means of production) developed in England prior to the seventeenth century, the lack of contribution of English economists to the theory and concept of entrepreneurship is conspicuous, especially before this century. Adam Smith, who wrote in 1776 at the time of the putting-out system and before the advent of the factory system, does not distinguish between entrepreneurs and capitalists, referring to "three different orders of people; . . .those who live by rent, . . .those who live by wages, and . . .those who live by profits" (i.e., employers, who receive profits from capital stock). Accordingly, he attributes the net income of a proprietor to returns for labor and capital (including a premium for risk), and does not allow any returns for direction and organization.[4]

Although Smith had no clear conception of the entrepreneurial function, he placed much stress on the importance of the business class. He believed that each individual would unwittingly add to wealth and welfare by furthering his own selfish ends.

In part, perhaps because of the authority of Smith, the classical economists of the early nineteenth century merged the entrepreneurial and capitalist functions, and failed to develop a theory on the differentiation between interests and profits. The classical school did not have an adequate concept of the entrepreneur: first, because of the inadequacy of the English language (eventually the term had to be borrowed from the French); second, they lacked an adequate theory of distribution which included the entrepreneur since they had no theory of general equilibrium, unlike the French economists, such as Richard Cantillon and Francis Quesnay; third, their belief that economic relationships are determined by natural law may have precluded an emphasis upon a conscious agent, such as the entrepreneur, at the center of the economic process.[5]

Alfred Marshall—The Distinction between Undertaker and Capitalist

Marshall distinguished between interest and the earnings of management (or the undertaker), indicating that these are what remain of profits after capital has been deducted. The business undertakers, who bring together the capital and labor required for the work, arrange the general plan, and superintend its minor details, may range from a highly skilled industrial worker (such as a foreman) to the top management official of the firm. Undertakers at one level of the hierarchy will be substituted for those at another level, as variations take place in the ratios of the marginal product to the wage rate among the different levels of the management organization. The undertakers who do not follow beaten tracks increase their earnings by introducing new and improved methods which result in copying by competitors. As a result, the earnings of the initial undertakers are decreased to what they were prior to the improvements.[6] This idea, not fully developed, is a premonition of Schumpeter's theory of innovation.

Leon Walras—The Entrepreneur as Coordinator of the Factors of Production

Walras, whose theory of general equilibrium in the last part of the nineteenth century has yet to be surpassed, designated the entrepreneur as the fourth factor of production who hires the others—land, labor, and capital.

The entrepreneur appears as buyer on the market for productive services, and the seller on the market for goods. Under free competition, the entrepreneur, in his role as a profit maximizer, is crucial in insuring that markets move toward an equilibrium. He enters branches of production which are profitable, thus increasing their output and eliminating profits (above competitive returns to the factors of production); and leaves industries incurring losses, thus decreasing the output of these goods and erasing losses.[7]

Joseph A. Schumpeter—The Entrepreneur as Innovator

It is a paradox that the English classical economists feared eventual stagnation despite the demonstrated ability of scientific discoveries and technical change to multiply output. In fact, it can be argued that the rapid economic growth of the Western world during the past century is essentially a story of how novel and vastly improved ways of satisfying wants were discovered and adopted. Professional economists have paid little systematic attention to the process of innovation—the embodiment in commercial practice of some new idea or invention—and to the innovator.[8]

One exception, Schumpeter, probably the major contributor to the literature on the conceptualization of the entrepreneur, linked innovation to the entrepreneur, maintained that the source of private profits is successful innovation, and contended that innovation is the essence of the development process. The entrepreneur is an innovator, one who carries out new combinations. These include five cases: (1) the introduction of a new good; (2) the introduction of a new production function; (3) the opening of a new market; (4) the conquest of a new source of supply of materials; and (5) the carrying out of a new organization of an industry.[9]

The Schumpeterian pure model begins with a circular flow (similar to a stationary state), an unchanging economic process which merely reproduces itself at constant rates in a closed domain, with an absence of innovators or entrepreneurs. This model, which assumes perfect competition, full employment, no capital accumulation, and no technical change, helps bring out in a clearer way the impact of the entrance of entrepreneurs. No entrepreneurial function is required, since the ordinary routine work, the repetition of orders and operations, can be done even by workmen.[10]

Into this flow, an entrepreneur motivated by money profits introduces an innovation consisting of a new production function which raises the marginal productivity of the various factors of production. Innovations generally involve the construction of new plants, and are embodied in a new firm, which implies the rise to leadership of new men. The orthodox assumption that business behavior is ideally rational and prompt, and is similar for all firms, is appropriate within the precincts of tried experience and familiar motive, but breaks down when the business community encounters "new possibilities of business action which are as yet untried and about which the most complete command of routine teaches nothing."[11]

The innovator differs from the manager of a firm, who runs the business on established lines. The entrepreneur is the engineer of change, not its product. It is difficult to identify him in practice, since no one acts exclusively as an entrepreneur. Though frequently he will be found among heads or founders of firms and/or among the major owners or stockholders, he need not necessarily hold a high official post in the firm, nor furnish capital or bear risks. Entrepreneurs arise from all economic classes.[12]

In the stationary economy, there may be high earnings for management, monopoly gains, windfalls, or speculative gains, but there are no entrepreneurial profits. Profits are the premium for innovation, and arise from no other source. Innovation however, sets up only a temporary monopoly gain, which is soon wiped out by imitation; for profits to continue, it is necessary to keep one step ahead of rivals with innovations. Profits result from the activities of the entrepreneur, even though they may not accrue to him in certain institutional settings.[13]

The creation of bank credit is initially associated with innovation, a breaking of the circular flow by the entrepreneur. Once a new production function has been successfully set up, imitation becomes easier for competitors. Thus, innovations are not isolated events evenly distributed in time, place, and sector; they tend to arise in clusters, as a result of varying incidences of risk. Eventually, the wave of entrepreneurial activity not only forces out old firms, but exhausts the limited possibilities of gain from the innovation. As borrowing diminishes, and loans are repaid, entrepreneurial activity tends to slacken and finally ceases. The differential rates of innovation and credit creation are the basis for Schumpeter's theory of the business cycle. The innovation, together with credit creation and saving, gives rise to economic growth.[14]

Schumpeter admits that his model is based on some very specific institutional assumptions and a specific historical context. It presupposes a capitalist society, with private property, private initiative, a money and banking system, a spirit of industrial bourgeoisie, and a scheme of motivation characterized by the nineteenth century in advanced economies prior to the era of Trustified Capitalism.[15]

In Schumpeter's well-integrated theory of economic growth, it is the entrepreneur as innovator, at the center of the model, that serves to explain the working of other variables in the system. But like a spark plug that is made to fit one machine, it is difficult to put the Schumpeterian entrepreneur into any other model of economic development. The fact that subsequent scholars have felt compelled to choose between the acceptance of the whole Schumpeterian system or the development of a different system probably explains why few students of entrepreneurship are disciples of Schumpeter.[16]

I want to evaluate Schumpeter's theory primarily as it relates to the question of entrepreneurship in less-developed economies. In the first place, the theory is purported to have validity only in capitalist economies prior to the rise of giant corporations. This may make it even less appropriate for underdeveloped capitalistic economies, since many industries in these countries, especially in manufacturing, are characterized by the dominance of a few large firms. Second, it is not clear why there needs to be a one-to-one correspondence between new innovations and the creation of new credit. Third, it seems unrealistic to preclude the possibility that innovations may result in the expansion of firms already existing. In fact, in the real world, characterized by imperfect competition, an organization with some time dimension might have an advantage in the development of new techniques, markets, products, and organizations. In the fourth place, Schumpeter does not incorporate a premium for risk into his theory of distribution. Fifth, it is difficult to test the theory empirically. Though the entrepreneurial function is clear, the persons performing the function cannot be readily identified. Furthermore, the impact of an initial innovation that starts growth and fluctuations is so swamped by the secondary and tertiary effects of the model that it is virtually impossible either to demonstrate or refute the hypothesis that innovations are the source of business cycles and economic development. Finally, the Schumpeterian model has only limited applicability to less-developed countries, as I argue below in my discussion of the concept of the entrepreneur adopted in this study.

The Distinction between Invention and Innovation

An invention needs to be put into business practice in order to become an innovation. History is replete with examples of inventions which occurred independently of any practical need, or which, more frequently, failed to obtain a sponsor or market. For example, Arthur H. Cole contends that the Stanley Steamer automobile in the United States in the early part of the twentieth century failed not because it was inferior to the automobile with the internal combustion engine, but because of the lack of an attempt at mass production by the Stanley brothers.[17]

W. Robert Maclaurin breaks down the elements of technical advance into (1) the development of pure science; (2) the invention; (3) the innovation; (4) the financing of the innovation; and (5) the acceptance of the innovation.[18] It is reassuring to low-income countries to know that frequently steps (1) and (2), and sometimes even (3), can be skipped, so that scarce high-level manpower can be devoted to the adaptation to business practice of discoveries already made. Perhaps these countries need to put more emphasis on institutions facilitating the financing and acceptance of promising innovations.

Frank Knight—The Entrepreneur as Decision-Maker under Conditions of Risk

To Knight, entrepreneurs bear the responsibility and the consequences of making decisions under conditions of uncertainty, that is, where the uniqueness of the situation denies an objective, quantitatively determinate probability. In such situations, the uncertainty cannot be eliminated by creating structures which consolidate or group a number of situations, by selecting specialized institutions (such as insurance companies) to bear the risk, by controlling the future (through overwhelming market power), by accurate power of prediction (through incurring costs of obtaining data), or by diffusion among a number of parties. However, where a risk can be computed, some of these methods can be used to reduce the uncertainty.[19]

To show the impact of uncertainty upon the profits of entrepreneurs, Knight analyzes the case where every member of the competitive system is virtually omniscient. In this situation, even though change may take place, profits are absent, since with complete foreknowledge, competition adjusts things to the point where all prices would equal costs. When omniscient firms foresee potential losses, they exit the industry until losses are removed; when profits are foreseen, all-knowing firms enter the industry until the point where the increased supply erases profits.[20]

In the state where all men have perfect knowledge of the future, there are no entrepreneurs, but only laborers performing the purely routine functions of reacting in mechanical fashion to data concerning the future. However, in a world of uncertainty, the entrepreneur, a new economic functionary endowed with knowledge, judgment, foresight, confidence in his own judgment, and capacity for ruling others, is required. As the person responsible for decisions in instances where there is unmeasurable uncertainty, the entrepreneur can make profits, since the lack of perfect foreknowledge prevents the perfect adjustment of supply by competitors to a no-profit equilibrium.[21]

Knight's entrepreneur bears the risk, a function which Schumpeter explicitly indicates belongs to the capitalist. The ultimate decision making and control in the firm lie with the risk bearer and not with the hired manager, even though he may be the managing director or chairman of the board of directors. Generally, it is not possible for a person to exercise only the function of entrepreneurship in the firm. The nearest case to this would be a man who borrowed all the resources for operating a firm (i.e., took the risk) and then hired a manager who was given a completely free hand. [22]

In Knight's view, it is fruitless to try to separate profit from interst, since the entrepreneur, almost of necessity, owns property. Profit is a residual share of income which falls to the person in *responsible* control of business, who generally also receives property income.

In contrast to Schumpeter's thesis, Knight's explanation has the advantage of making profit a return to the function of entrepreneurship. However, there is no reason why the reward to the entrepreneur needs to be in the form of profits in all institutional settings. Most economists would contend that the control of the giant corporation in the United States today is generally not in the hands of the stockholders but of management, which in many cases is self-perpetuating. Where this is true, Knight's contention that the persons who exercise the function of control in the firm also bear risk can be questioned.

Maurice Dobb—The Entrepreneur as Innovator, Risk-Taker and Monopolist

Dobb acknowledges that any society with modern machine techniques and extensive division of labor requires some coordinating, controlling, or integrating force, which is, he indicates, the entrepreneurial function. The principal elements of this function, a synthesis of the concepts of Schumpeter and Knight, are the capacity for adjustment and innovation, which includes, most importantly, the ability to make correct judgments about the future.[23]

The capitalist undertaker, who usually also plays the role of the capitalist, generally obtains profits as a result of some monopoly advantage. This fact does not mean that he inhibits economic progress, nor that the situation is necessarily morally undesirable. The monopoly or advantage that the undertaker exploits, except that which results from inherent ability, is the result of the possession of greater opportunities such as (1) greater information; (2) superior access to training and education; (3) a lower discount of future earnings; (4) greater firm size; and (5) agreements to restrict entry or output. All five are facilitated by the possession of wealth or position. An elaboration of these advantages to the capitalist entrepreneur is a basis for my discussion in chapter 4 of the lack of upward socioeconomic mobility in entrepreneurship.

For Dobb, capitalist undertaking in conditions of some monopoly privilege is par excellence a progressive force, as indicated by the economic growth of the hundred years prior to 1926 (when he was writing). Few persons are willing to face the burden of uncertainty in an environment where they have little control. The head of a large capitalist corporation or a communist planning board is more likely to commit large resources to expanding output than is a small enterprise in a freely competitive economy.[24]

Despite the success of capitalism in the past century, Dobb questions whether it can, in the future, with the rise of trusts and imperialism, satisfy the demands of economic adjustment and income distribution more effectively than communism. Economic theory cannot help us very much with this problem, he continues, without new approaches, since the theory of capitalist undertaking is, as of 1926, primarily based on the assumption of a society of classless individualism.[25] Despite the analysis of imperfect competition by Joan Robinson and Edward Chamberlain in the following decade, much of Dobb's criticism of economic theory is still valid.

THE ENTREPRENEUR IN CONTEMPORARY ECONOMIC THEORY

Despite the large number of historical and empirical studies on entrepreneurship in the last three decades, it is safe to say, as William J. Baumol does, that the entrepreneur has about disappeared from the current theoretical literature in economics. Baumol attributes this primarily to the fact that our microeconomic models are instruments of the analysis of optimality in well-defined problems where the variables are also well defined—that is, these are problems which need no entrepreneur for their solution. A person with exceptional vision of the future obviously cannot fit into most current microeconomic models, in which, Baumol suggests, the businessman is a maximizing automaton. Furthermore, the entrepreneur has not been defined in an empirically meaningful manner, and thus is difficult to conceptualize.[26]

Harvey Leibenstein, in agreeing with Baumol, points out that the entrepreneur has only a trivial role in the type of models prevalent in present economic theory—static models which assume complete certainty.

> If all inputs are marketed and their prices are known, and if all outputs are marketed and their prices are known and if there is a definite production function that relates inputs to outputs in a determinate way, then we can always predict the profit for any activity that transforms inputs into outputs. If net profits are positive, then this should serve as a signal for entry into this market. The problems of marshaling resources and turning them into outputs appears to be a trivial activity. From this point of view it is hard to see why there should ever be a deficiency of entrepreneurship. The answer is that the standard competitive model hides the vital function of the entrepreneur.[27]

Leibenstein, in his theory of entrepreneurship, elaborates on the distinction between Schumpeterian or N-entrepreneurship, and routine management. N-entrepreneurship indicates the activities essential "to create or carry on an enterprise where not all the markets are well established or clearly defined" and/or in which the relevant parts of the production function are not fully specified and completely known.

According to Leibenstein, an entrepreneur is an individual or group of individuals with four main characteristics. First, "he is capable of making up for market deficiencies (gap filling)," a capability which is scarce. There is no one-to-one correspondence between sets of inputs and outputs. Since individuals and firms do not work as effectively, search for new information and techniques as diligently, and maintain constant effort at as high a level as they could, many firms operate with a considerable degree of slack. Furthermore, frequently, especially in less-developed countries, inputs in the production function are not well defined, and there is not a well-developed market for them. The entrepreneur may need to possess some of the capacities to search, discover, and evaluate economic opportunities; marshall financial resources and undertake management responsibility for the firm; and acquire new economic information and translate it into new markets, techniques, and products, since these attributes are frequently unmarketed or difficult to market. To illustrate, if a certain type of machine has to be employed to produce a particular type of commodity, if no one in the country produces the machine, and if imports are barred, then only entrepreneurs who have access to information on how to construct the machine can enter the industry.

Second, the entrepreneur has the ability to connect different markets, that is, the skill to obtain and use factors of production that are not well marketed. For example, in order to insure that he is not faced with a crucial bottleneck in the matrix of information, finance, markets, and inputs required, the entrepreneur may need political and family connections.

Third, the entrepreneur must be an "input completer." For any given economic activity, there is a minimum quantity of inputs that must be marshaled. If less than this minimum is available, the entrepreneur has the job of stepping in to fill the lack of marketable inputs.

In the fourth place, the entrepreneur creates or expands firms. Unlike the prevailing theory, Leibenstein points out the importance of the existence of firms as time-binding entities. Since the production function is not complete, firms become valuable storehouses of detailed knowledge and experience. Because of the time duration of the firm, it can capture some of the long-term advantages of previous gap filling and input completing.[28]

Furthermore, Leibenstein contends, the entrepreneur as gap-filler and input-completer is probably the prime mover in shifts to more productive techniques, the accumulation of new knowledge, the creation or adoption of new goods, new markets, new materials, new organizational forms, and the creation of new skills—important elements in the process of economic growth. The works of Solow, Abramovitz, and others[29] have shown that growth cannot be explained by increases in standard inputs, such as labor and capital. The existence of and necessity for gap filling and input completing could help to explain why these inputs do not account for all outputs. The lack of a fixed relationship between inputs and outputs is partly explained by the fact that entrepreneurship is not a normal input whose contribution can be readily determined, predicted, planned for, or controlled.

The demand for entrepreneurs is determined by the potential opportunities for gap fillers and input completers, namely, the difference between the techniques and inputs corresponding to the maximum production possibilities available in the world, the subset of techniques known in detail by a routine search, and the inputs needed for production which are marketed on a routine basis.

The demand for entrepreneurs is determined by the extent to which gap filling and input completing can increase production beyond the level at which techniques are widely available and inputs are routinely marketed. The supply of entrepreneurs is determined by the availability of persons with gap-filling and input-completing capacities, and the social, political, and motivational factors which influence the extent to which individuals utilize these capacities.[30]

Empiricists and historians, in comparison to theorists, are far more willing to give the entrepreneur a central place in economic history and development. Despite this, Soltow argues, the large number of studies in U.S. business theory in the 1930s, 1940s, and 1950s, and the few empirical studies of entrepreneurship in less-developed countries in recent years have added little clarity to the theory of the role and function of entrepreneurship or the theory of the relationship between entrepreneurship and economic development.[31] In general, there has been little feedback between these studies and the small number of theoretical works which have incorporated the entrepreneur into their scheme.

THE MULTIPLE ENTREPRENEURIAL FUNCTION

With the increased complexity of business organizations today as a result of technical change, the question may be raised as to whether several persons within a firm may exercise the entrepreneurial function. Though some writers imply a multiple exercise of the entrepreneurial function, this has generally not been discussed explicitly. Until recent years, when a few writers have discussed the idea of plural entrepreneurship, there has been little recognition of the problem.[32]

Frederick Harbison finds it useful to consider the entrepreneur as "an *organization* which comprises all the people required to perform the entrepreneurial functions." These functions consist of (1) the undertaking or managing of risk and the handling of economic uncertainty; (2) planning and innovation; (3) coordination, administration and control; and (4) routine supervision. Although in the very small enterprise, the functions may all be performed by one person, the proprietor, in large establishments there may be a division of functions among a complex hierarchy of individuals. Harbison suggests that the aggregation of persons bearing the entrepreneurial function might more appropriately be labeled "organization" rather than "the entrepreneur." Organization connotes not only the constellation of functions, persons and abilities used in the management of the enterprise, but also the nature of the integration of these into a common undertaking. The concept of organization has the advantage of being subject to quantitative measurement, making it possible to consider the idea of "investment in organization" in the same terms as "investment in machinery or equipment," and "accumulation of managerial resources" as a concept parallel to capital accumulation.[33] In large joint-stock companies, where those undertaking the entrepreneurial role may be difficult to identify, there may be advantages to using the concept of organization rather than that of the entrepreneur in the analysis of the functions of coordination, planning, innovation, and risk bearing.

In his study of Indian entrepreneurship, Pritam Singh uses a concept similar to Harbison. According to Singh, entrepreneurship involves the actual creation or extension of an organization or institution, which gives rise to various growth-producing phenomena such as increases in productivity, technical change, saving, and investment. The objectives of the organization the entrepreneurs build may be either social service or profit making, giving the concept an applicability to the public sector of capitalistic economies or to centrally planned economies.[34]

THE MANAGEMENT AND ENTREPRENEURIAL FUNCTIONS

What is the difference between the management function and the entrepreneurial function? Students of entrepreneurship, following the Schumpeterian definition, have tended to indicate that the management function is to manage the continuing operation of a firm, or to administer and oversee the day-to-day process of production in which combinations carried out in the past are simply repeated or subject to routine adaptations. The entrepreneurial function consists of doing things not generally done in the ordinary course of business routine. The entrepreneur makes decisions under conditions of uncertainty where problems are not well defined. Entrepreneurs may be found among owners and equity holders; boards of directors; management officials; professional, technical, and supervisory personnel; creditors and bankers; outside advisors; and others. The decisions of entrepreneurs require a creative response, as opposed to merely a routine or adaptive response required of managers.[35]

In recent years, economists concerned about identification of the entrepreneur in empirical studies have been more prone than in the past to broaden the concept of the entrepreneur to include management of the continuing operation of the firm. In a changing economy, it is difficult to draw a line between the adaptations of day-to-day management and the innovative and creative decisions of the entrepreneur.

THE CONCEPT OF THE ENTREPRENEUR USED IN THIS STUDY

From among the various concepts of the entrepreneur suggested, it is necessary to find one that is not only satisfactory theoretically, but can also be used empirically in a field study in less-developed countries. The entrepreneur is conceptualized in at least three major ways in the orthodox literature in economics: as the fourth factor of production who coordinates and hires the others (Walras), as the innovator, that is, the one who carries out new combinations (Schumpeter), and as the ultimate decision maker in the enterprise, the one who commits the capital and bears the risk (Knight). Although each of these concepts has advantages for particular purposes, in this study I have used a concept similar to Knight's.

The Walrasian definition has advantages for the theory of general equilibrium, which discusses the role of the entrepreneur as a profit maximizer entering and leaving the industry. However, for field study purposes, this concept is too vague to use in identifying the personnel in a firm who coordinate and hire land, labor, and capital.

In most less-developed countries, the role of the Schumpeterian entrepreneur is somewhat limited. A large number of indigenous Schumpeterian entrepreneurs are trading entrepreneurs whose innovations are the opening of new markets. In light of the possibilities of technical transfer from advanced economies, no undue emphasis should be put on the development of entirely new combinations.

Furthermore, the alternative potential of technical, executive, and organizational skills in underdeveloped economies may be too high to allow their use in developing new combinations in the Schumpeterian sense. Usually, fewer high-level skills are expended if combinations are adapted from economically advanced countries.[36]

Schumpeter's concept of the entrepreneur could be broadened to include those who adapt and modify already existing innovations.[37] However, it is not possible to translate this concept into a working definition which would enable other investigators to concur in the identification of entrepreneurs. Most business activity in a nonstationary state involves the necessity of some innovation, since each firm faces unique factors (most obviously, location and date of establishment). A firm's economic setting, in addition, changes over time. Absolute imitation is therefore impossible, and techniques developed outside the firm must be adapted to its own circumstances. This is especially true in the case of a firm in a less-developed country borrowing technology from an advanced economy with different relative factor prices—for example, a higher price of labor relative to capital. These adaptations require innovation, if "innovation" is used in a less restrictive sense than Schumpeter used it.[38] However, this modification of the Schumpeterian framework has not proved workable in practice. Two independent field researchers would not be able to agree upon innovations and innovators within a given universe of firms.[39] Moreover, the entrepreneur, in the modified Schumpeterian framework, is no longer very distinctive among businessmen.

This study uses a concept similar to Knight's, in which the entrepreneur is the ultimate decision maker in the enterprise. It is he, and not the hired manager, who commits the (ownership) capital and bears the risks.[40] During our interviews, my colleagues and I could obtain information on the distribution of initial ownership holdings within the firm. However, in some instances, more than one person owned capital within the firm. To cope with the problem of identifying quantities of entrepreneurship, it is assumed that there is one unit—the entrepreneur—in each firm. The entrepreneur is identified as the person with the largest initial capital share in the enterprise (or where these shares are equal, the person with the principal responsibility for making the decision to commit the capital to the firm).[41]

I am not implying that Knight's concept would be the most appropriate for all empirical research on entrepreneurship. For example, his definition may not be suitable for studies of the giant joint-stock company, where the functions of ownership and control are usually separate, and are generally exercised by a large number of persons.

In practice, in small firms, there is probably not much difference between the entrepreneur in the frameworks of Knight and Walras. In one-man and family enterprises, he who commits the capital and bears the risk (Knight's entrepreneur) is likely also to be the coordinator and hirer of capital, labor, and land (the Walrasian concept). On the other hand, only a few of those considered entrepreneurs according to Knight's definition would be regarded as entrepreneurs in Schumpeter's framework. Even if the Schumpeterian concept is broadened to include as an innovator one who carries out "new combinations" in the coastal Andhran economy, not all entrepreneurs in this study would be considered to be Schumpeterian entrepreneurs.[42]

CONTEMPORARY EMPIRICAL STUDIES OF ENTREPRENEURS IN LESS-DEVELOPED ECONOMIES

Since others have reviewed the literature on entrepreneurship in less-developed economies, this section can be briefer and more selective. Harris' survey of empirical studies of entrepreneurship, primarily in poor countries, is the most comprehensive available.[43] Kilby's discussion of various perspectives on entrepreneurship is not as exhaustive as the Harris survey, but emphasizes the correlation of the theoretical literature from a large number of disciplines with the existing empirical literature.[44] Here I focus on six of the leading contemporary studies of industrial entrepreneurship in less-developed countries which acquire data through the use of interviews—Sayigh's study of Lebanon,[45] Carroll's on the Philippines,[46] Alexander's on Greece,[47] Papanek's on Pakistan,[48] and works by Nafziger[49] and Harris[50] on Nigeria. Another major empirical study, that by Berna on Tamil Nadu, India,[51] is included in the next chapter, a survey of work on Indian entrepreneurship. Since these studies are included in the discussion by Harris and Kilby, my purpose is merely to emphasize aspects of the works that introduce issues relevant to an understanding of this study.

Sayigh, in his survey of 207 Lebanese entrepreneurs in 1959, carefully develops his conceptual framework and designs his questions so as to test hypotheses made by economists in the theoretical literature on entrepreneurship. In a manner similar to Schumpeter, Sayigh identifies increases in the productive capacity of an economy with the application of innovative enterprise to advances in technology. However, Schumpeter's entrepreneur is broadened to include the derivation or adaptation of innovations. Furthermore, unlike Schumpeter, the innovation need not be embodied in a new firm, but might be the basis for building or improving "an organization capable of successfully promoting the [innovative] idea and assuring the businessman a position of leadership in the field." In his search for entrepreneurs to study, Sayigh relied on files from public and semipublic bodies; chambers of commerce, industry, and agriculture; and industrial associations to aid in the selection of innovators in the manufacturing, agricultural, financial, and services sectors.[52]

In Lebanon, Christians constitute a disproportionate share of innovating entrepreneurs, four-fifths, as compared to only one-half of the general population. On the other hand, only one-sixth of the entrepreneurial group is Muslim compared to 44 percent of the population as a whole. The recent national origin (i.e., that of the father of the respondent at the time of his birth) of 72 percent of the entrepreneurs was Lebanese, and 7 percent each Palestinian and Armenian. More than 70 percent of the business leaders had travelled outside their country of origin before starting their present business careers.

Sayigh, who finds that less than one-fourth of the entrepreneurs are engaged in the same sector as their father, stresses the "remarkable mobility between generations." Thirty-one percent of the fathers were in trade, 26 percent in industry, and 9 percent in the professions. The major occupation of entrepreneurs prior to their present activity was trade, which together with industry comprised about two-thirds of the previous occupations of respondents. In addition, apparently they perceived their own economic and social statuses as higher than those of their fathers.[53]

Carroll's 1960 survey of ninety-two indigenous industrial entrepreneurs in the Philippines in establishments with more than ninety-nine employed has the most detailed analysis of the socioeconomic background and mobility of the entrepreneurs. The differences between the actual representation of entrepreneurs by ethnic and geographical origins and origin by size of city, on the one hand, and the expected representation based on population, on the other, are highly significant. Carroll, in explaining why entrepreneurs are disproportionately from big cities, suggests that their culture creates the need and awareness of the possibility of entrepreneurial success, without considering the possibility that those located in the cities have greater access to business opportunities. A majority of the fathers of the entrepreneurs, and the respondents themselves immediately before their present activity, bore or shared chief responsibility for the management of at least one enterprise. Although entrepreneurs whose fathers were of the upper stratum are tremendously overrepresented among the sample group, a substantial majority of the fathers was not of the upper stratum. Increasingly after 1950, with greater financial and skill barriers to business activity, entrepreneurship has become a means of enhancing or consolidating an upper status position already possessed. Yet, Carroll argues that in the final analysis, "mobility was quite dramatically evident," and "there has been, in fact, a very impressive amount of mobility in the family of the entrepreneurs."[54]

Alexander's 1961 study of 354 Greek industrialists in establishments with fifty or more workers, although based on a self-selected sample obtained by a mail questionnaire, tries to focus on "questions concerning the supply of entrepreneurs and the nature of their policies."[55] Despite a deliberate government policy to protect domestic industrial production, economic opportunities in manufacturing were relatively less attractive than in trade because of a small domestic market, the absence of a capital market for industrialists, and the lack of availability of industrial management skills. In the Greek sample, as in Alexander's previous study of Turkish entrepreneurs,[56] big merchants are most highly overrepresented. Former craftsmen, especially well represented in the early phases of industrialization, tended to have less drive and vision, and directed relatively small firms. Greek refugees, resulting from the exchange of minorities between Turkey and Greece in the 1920s, were especially well represented among entrepreneurs. Alexander argues that there is considerable upward mobility in entrepreneurial activity, and a lack of sharp class demarcation, partly because feudal-aristocratic survivals are weak in Greece.

Papanek studied 250 industrialists employing twenty or more workers in Pakistan, a country with substantial industrial growth between independence in 1947 and the time of the study, 1959. As a result of India-Pakistan partition at independence, vast opportunities opened up for the Muslim business community, because of the separation from Indian industry and the exodus of the dominant Hindu businessman. The government, through protection of domestic production, subsidization by undervaluation of foreign exchange, and industrial incentive programs, such as generous depreciation allowances, increased the rate of return of manufacturing relative to trade, and stimulated the development of industrial entrepreneurship. Forty-three percent of Muslim industrialists were members of the Halai Memon, Chinioti, Dawoodi Bohra, Khoja Ismaili, and Khoja Isnashari communities, which altogether account for less than one-half percent of the Pakistani population. The previous primary occupation of 45 percent of the industrialists was trade. Papanek argues that the findings of his study lend support to the thesis that entrepreneurship in manufacturing arises in response to powerful economic incentives rather than significant changes in sociopsychological variables.[57] However, as Hagen maintains, Papanek provides no information concerning child-rearing practices and personality, and the evidence available concerning the small trading communities from which the entrepreneurs originated tends to suggest the possibility of substantial sociopsychological changes.[58]

My study of ninety Nigerian footwear manufacturing entrepreneurs, interviewed in 1964–65, focuses on an analysis of factors related to the number and success of entrepreneurs. Major criteria for entrepreneurial success are level and growth of output and rate of profit as ascertained from the records of the firms. The scarcity of Nigerian entrepreneurs results from a combination of the paucity of demand (i.e., impediments in the economic environment, partly arising from the colonial legacy) and the lack of supply (i.e., deficiencies of appropriate technical, managerial, and organizational skills because of insufficient training, education, and experience and a lack of sociocultural milieu conducive to the development of entrepreneurship). The analysis of the market for entrepreneurs is useful in the designing of training programs for businessmen. For example, the demand for skilled persons is so keen that the graduates of small-scale industrial training institutes have alternatives that are too attractive for them to continue to choose entrepreneurial positions in small firms.[59]

Because time and money spent for formal education represent relinquished opportunities in training more closely related to entrepreneurial occupations, the education of the entrepreneur is negatively related to the profit rate of his firm. In addition, with the brisk demand for educated persons in foreign enterprises and the civil service, those with

a university or secondary education are likely to have chosen an entrepreneurial pursuit because of failure in another occupation or low opportunity costs. However, education and literacy of the entrepreneur
do set a limit to the size and complexity of the firm.[60]

Although the extended family hinders the expansion of the firm by
diverting resources for current consumption which might otherwise
have been reinvested in business, the family facilitates entry into entrepreneurial positions by providing funds for apprentice training and
initial capital.[61]

There is almost no interregional migration among Nigerian manufacturing entrepreneurs. In addition to barriers of language, culture,
and communal discrimination, a major reason is the lack of political
and economic security of businessmen in other communal group
areas. Interregional differences in return to entrepreneurship persist
because of barriers to migration.[62]

In 1965 Harris conducted a study of 269 Nigerian entrepreneurs,
primarily in the sawmilling, furniture, rubber processing, printing,
garment-making, and baking industries. Nigerian entrepreneurs have
been geographically immobile as only five of the entrepreneurs were
operating businesses outside of their region of birth. He finds that
"entrepreneurial activity is a means of moving one or two 'notches up
the ladder,' " as the occupational and socioeconomic statuses of the
businessmen are higher than those of their fathers.[63]

Nigerian entrepreneurs have been somewhat successful in identifying opportunities and gaining command over resources, but relatively
unsuccessful in the management of enterprises they have founded.
The Ibo and Yoruba ethnic communities are disproportionately represented among industrial entrepreneurs, and the Hausa-Fulani underrepresented, consistent with predictions based on LeVine's study of
communal differences in achievement motivation.[64]

THE CONTRIBUTION OF THIS STUDY

Chapter 1 discussed the contribution of the study. Let me elaborate
somewhat by focusing on the major similarities and differences between this study and the empirical studies reviewed. The present
study, like the others, analyzes information on the education and
training, occupational and socioeconomic background, communal
origin, sources of initial capital, and relationship to government of the
entrepreneurs.

However, there are three major ways in which this study can be distinguished from empirical studies by other authors. First, the study examines data on entrepreneurial participation, success, and behavior, not only in light of the impact of entrepreneurship upon economic growth, but also from the perspective of the distribution of entrepreneurial opportunities within the population. Thus, the most important contribution of the study is its emphasis upon the representation of various segments of the population in entrepreneurial activity, particularly the difference in representation between the privileged and underprivileged portions of the population. In this study, data on the distribution of entrepreneurs by class (parental economic and occupational status) and caste are compared with information on the population at large, and are related to the educational attainment, entrepreneurial and managerial experience, initial capital, access to government assistance, and business success of the entrepreneurs. Except for Carroll's reference[65] to the disproportionate representation of fathers of entrepreneurs in upper socioeconomic positions, none of the other authors takes note of the differences in class origins of entrepreneurs as opposed to the population as a whole. However, as I have indicated in the last chapter, in the studies of Harris and Alexander, enough information is available, even though not discussed explicitly, for the reader interested in an analysis of class differentials between entrepreneurs and the general population to make certain inferences. On a related point, the survey of studies of Indian entrepreneurship in chapter 3 indicates that, though some authors discuss the caste origin of entrepreneurs, none has the statistical information available to compare the caste representation of entrepreneurs with that of the general population.

A second point, related to the first, is that most of the works by other authors are less comprehensive in obtaining data to compare characteristics of entrepreneurs and the population as a whole. In my study of Nigerian entrepreneurs, I obtained information to compare the ethnic origin, sector of occupational origin, sector of paternal occupational origin, educational attainment, median personal income, and region of birth to those of the population at large. Here I have the same comparative data in addition to those on caste and paternal economic status. Harris contrasted the paternal occupation, ethnic origin, and educational background of the entrepreneurs to the population. Alexander obtained comparative data on occupational origin, size of city of birth, and level of education. Carroll was able to compare the differences between the actual representation of entrepreneurs by the sectors of their previous occupation and that of their father, by ethnic and geographical origin, and by origin by size of city, on the one hand, with the expected representation based on population, on the other. Papanek compared communal origins of entrepreneurs with the population as a whole, and Sayigh, the religious affiliation of businessmen to the general population.

Third, few of the other studies have access to measures of the success or performance of the entrepreneurs, such as their income class and the gross value added of their firms.[66] Furthermore, some of the investigators who do have access to indicators of success fail to correlate these with the socioeconomic characteristics of the entrepreneurs. Factors related to business success are found by correlating these measures of success with caste, class, education, work background, sources and amounts of initial capital, and access to government. Harris' indices of success were employment, a measure of input rather than output or value added, and degree of "success of the firm," an index which is not explicitly defined or subject to replication by other investigators.[67] These indices of success were related to the occupations of the fathers and grandfathers, and the occupational origin, ethnic origin, and educational level of the entrepreneur. While Papanek did not have an explicit indicator of business success, he did compare the reasons for entrance into industry by entrepreneurs in large firms with entrepreneurs in general. Alexander obtained figures on the size of firm by employment, but did not analyze socioeconomic factors related to the size of the entrepreneurs' firms. Although Carroll had data on employment and paid-up capital, both inputs, he did not relate these to the socioeconomic attachments of the entrepreneurs. Sayigh, on the other hand, had no indicators of entrepreneurial success.

SUMMARY

The entrepreneur is conceptualized in at least three major ways in the literature in economics: (1) as the coordinator of resources of production; (2) as the innovator; and (3) as the decision maker. For this study, I am using Knight's concept of the entrepreneur as the ultimate decision maker in the enterprise, the one who commits the capital and bears the risk.

The entrepreneur has just about disappeared from the contemporary theoretical literature in economics. Thus, the questions posed in this study tend to be drawn from earlier economic works, and the contemporary literature on social science, economic development, and some applied fields in economics.

Recent empirical studies on entrepreneurs in underdeveloped countries suggest a few issues of concern to this study—the communal origin, occupational background, and socioeconomic mobility of the entrepreneurs. However, most of these studies have not stressed several of the questions central here—the distribution of entrepreneurial activities between various classes and groups within the population and the factors related to the quantity and success of entrepreneurs.

3

STUDIES OF INDIAN ENTREPRENEURSHIP

THIS survey of the leading studies of Indian entrepreneurs is meant to introduce the reader to some of the major themes, issues, and controversies in the literature, and to provide a background sketch on the Indian economy and society essential to a study of indigenous entrepreneurs. The delineation of studies which belong in this review depends a great deal upon the judgment of the author. For example, a number of studies of small industry, whose major focus is not the entrepreneur, have not been included.

Students in the field of entrepreneurship benefit from the cross-fertilization of a wide number of disciplines and approaches. Studies of Indian entrepreneurship have been chosen from a number of fields in history and the social sciences. Reality is an unbroken totality, a seamless robe. The frequent tendency for social scientists, and especially economists, to consider only the fragment of social reality that lies within the scope of their professional discipline may detract from an understanding of socioeconomic phenomena rather than enhance comprehension. So although I am an economist, this review encompasses literature from a large number of disciplines.

A brief sketch of the history of Indian entrepreneurship is provided as a part of a general background to this study. Discussions of leading Indian business communities, previous empirical studies which analyze entrepreneurship and social community, and the relationship between caste and entrepreneurship help place my subsequent examination of socioeconomic origins of Vizag entrepreneurs in introductory and comparative perspective. An understanding of the role of the family (together with the community) in business activity enhances the reader's comprehension of entrepreneurs and their firms as a part of a wider social nexus. The present-day importance of country-wide industrial empires which maintain a "community of interest" between the principals of a number of firms can be understood more clearly as a result of an examination of the managing agency system, the dominant type of large business organization prior to 1970. Finally, the investigation of the use of achievement motivation training to heighten business activity in India suggests that the need for achievement may not be a primary variable, but merely a correlate of socioeconomic class, a determinant of entrepreneurship emphasized in my empirical study.

A HISTORICAL SKETCH OF INDIAN ENTREPRENEURSHIP
The Period Prior to this Century

Indian handicraft industries, such as textiles, enjoyed a worldwide reputation in ancient times, as attested by the use of Indian muslin in wrapping Egyptian mummies.[1] This sketch however, begins in the seventeenth and eighteenth centuries, the period corresponding to the early years of British influence. In 1750, India was as urbanized as England, France, and Italy, and as industrialized as Japan and most of eastern Europe. During the seventeenth century, there were a number of entrepreneurs in major trading areas in the Indus River Valley in northwestern India (much of which is presently a part of Pakistan), in northeastern India around the Ganges River and its tributaries, and in southern India's coastal areas which engaged in foreign trade. In addition, in the eighteenth century, Indian merchants, brokers, and company servants dealt with European privileged and chartered companies (such as the English East India Company). During the seventeenth and eighteenth centuries, Indians were involved as financiers—in changing money, providing bills of exchange, loaning to government, acting as treasurer and revenue collector for government, and loaning to private parties (including Europeans).[2]

By 1800 the factory system had been developed in England, and before 1825 the system had obtained a foothold in a few other Western countries. Although several English businessmen established factories in India in the first half of the nineteenth century, it was not until the middle of the century with the expansion of the market through the development of railways and other internal transport, that such manufacturing enterprises extended beyond initial ventures in a few industries. Around 1850, Indian industrial and financial entrepreneurs became involved, especially in western India, and were instrumental in the substantial progress in modern manufacturing during the last half of the nineteenth century.[3] At the same time, Indian handicrafts, which had had a wide reputation for a long time, declined as a result of the competition of machine-made goods at home and abroad, the development of new tastes, and the disappearance of the patronage of princely courts.[4] Probably the major Indian contribution in the nineteenth century came in the field of banking, where every company of any importance owed its existence, in part, to the enterprise and capital of Indians.[5]

The Twentieth Century

In the early part of this century, a few beginnings were made by Indians in heavy industry—steel, engineering, electric power, and shipping.[6] The most spectacular of these ventures was by Jamshedjee Tata, a Parsi, who was responsible for India's first viable steel enterprise in Jamshedpur in 1911.

Before World War I, government responsibility in economic affairs was confined primarily to the establishment of peace and justice, and the provision of basic public services. Although the Indian Industrial Commission, appointed in 1916, recommended that the government play an active role in the industrial development of the country, little initiative was taken by the central government. However, after the shortages of strategic goods during World War I, the United Kingdom recognized its interest in selective encouragement of industries in the colonies which did not threaten British manufacturers. Accordingly, the recommendation of the Fiscal Commission in 1921 did lead to the protection of certain industries such as iron and steel, cotton textiles, sugar, paper, matches, and heavy chemicals. Industrial development accelerated and diversified in the 1930s and 1940s, with indigenous enterprise increasingly setting the pace.

The rate of growth in industrial output increased in the first half of the twentieth century over that of the last half of the nineteenth century. Although industrial production doubled between 1912 and 1945,[7] industrial output per head grew by only about 1 percent per annum.

Most intellectuals and leaders in the nationalist movement were convinced that slow economic growth in the colonial period was largely the result of a policy of laissez-faire capitalism. The emphasis upon systematic state economic planning, to remove the deep-seated obstacles to development from the British era, was a part of the ideology of the nationalist movement.[8] In 1931, the Indian National Congress promised government ownership or control of industries in an independent India, while in 1938, a Congress committee studied state planning. When India received its independence in 1947, its leaders decided it was necessary for government to have a major role in the process of industrial development, through a gradual increase in the relative size of the public sector and through the use of physical controls to direct investment in the private sector. Particular emphasis was placed on the establishment of government enterprises to alleviate the lack of production of basic capital goods—a lack that was exacerbating the long run balance-of-payments problem. The share of net national product contributed by government enterprises grew from 2.8 percent in 1948/49 to 6.6 percent in 1965/66. Yet even after the Industrial Policy Resolution of 1956, which extended the number of basic and strategic industries in the public sector, the size of the public sector was not large. Government enterprises accounted for only 4 percent of the total working force (in 1957/58).[9]

Nevertheless, much of the major new industrial entrepreneurial activity in recent years has been in the public sector, which has accounted for over one-half of investment in manufacturing in the last decade. Although in some activities government investment has deterred private investment, in other instances government has stimulated demand for industry by investing in order to alleviate bottlenecks and by creating new linkages with other industries. The indigenous industrial entrepreneurial function has been facilitated by investment in social overhead capital, state-sponsored lending institutions, restrictions on foreign investment, increased protection of local industry, inducements to small-scale industries, and the formation of industrial estates. On the other hand, as indicated below, industrial licensing, price controls, administrative restrictions and regulations, and a highly progressive tax rate on income and wealth have hampered domestic entrepreneurship. Finally, since independence, industrialization has widened geographically as a result of the Industrial Policy Resolutions and plan documents stressing the need for balanced regional development.[10]

LEADING INDIAN BUSINESS COMMUNITIES
The Concept of Caste

Caste, together with regional and linguistic community, is used in the analysis of entrepreneurial activity in this study. Caste refers to the ancient four-rank *varna* system for Hindus—Brahmin (priest), Kshatriya (ruler and warrior), Vaishya (trader), and Sudra (artisan, peasant, and laborer), in addition to the "untouchables" (or Harijans); and religion in the case of the non-Hindu population: Sikhs, Muslims, Jains, Parsis, Christians, and a few others. The first three Hindu *varna* are twice-born castes (i.e., higher castes which have gone through a special ceremony in youth indicating a second or spiritual birth). More specific than the *varna* is the *jati*, which is still the basic kinship and social particle in a system of hierarchically arranged, locally integrated, occupationally and ritually specialized, endogamous social strata. Yet the concept of *varna*, recognized by the courts during the colonial period and supported by the leading castes to legitimize their status, has helped to shape social reality and is accepted by ordinary Indians as a conceptual device to understand the caste system.[11]

Caste is *not* an immutable system where the position of each *jati* is fixed throughout time. In the middle regions of the *varna* hierarchy, caste standing is at times vague and flexible. In fact, the Sudra categories range from powerful and rich *jati*s with a relatively high ritual status to those whose assimilation into Hinduism is only marginal. Some of the former Sudra *jati*s have been able to rise to a higher position in the *varna* hierarchy in a generation or two through Sanskritization (the adoption of the rituals of twice-born castes, Brahmins, Kshatriyas, and Vaishyas).[12]

Caste is used rather than *jati* for several reasons. First, caste is highly correlated with family socioeconomic status and class in India. In the second place, specialization in business activity and other economic functions frequently coincides with caste (and social community). Third, most of the studies reviewed in this chapter emphasize the wider definition of caste. In chapter 4 I indicate further why I use caste for the analysis of entrepreneurs in Andhra.

The Eighteenth and Nineteenth Centuries

In the eighteenth century, the Khatris and Lohanas, Hindu and Sikh communities in which caste divisions and rules were not rigidly observed, were the leading entrepreneurs in trade and finance in northwestern India, despite the fact that the ruling class and the bulk of the population were Muslims. Gujarat and Saurashtra had a highly developed Hindu and Jain[13] trading community, in addition to Muslim communities comprising converts from Hindu trading and artisan communities; later in the century an indigenous Parsi group became active in trade. In Maharashtra local Brahmins and trading classes from Gujarat, Rajasthan, Saurashtra, and Kutch dominated business. Hindu and Jain Banias (trading communities) from Rajasthan (the former state of Marwar and adjoining states), called Marwaris in other states, were the leading commercial and banking communities in northeastern India around the Ganges River. In Bengal indigenous Brahmins and Kayasthas, as a result of their positions as assistants and agents for the dominant British businessmen, obtained access to the major entrepreneurial positions instead of the Bengali trading classes. Various Hindu trading communities (such as the Chettis in Madras) dominated business in South India, except for Kerala where Muslims, Christians, and Jews were the chief traders.[14]

The Parsis, primarily agriculturalists in the seventeenth century, became the leading Indian business community in the first half of the nineteenth century, with a number of sizeable ventures in raw cotton and opium trade, shipbuilding, banking, printing, and other endeavors. They, together with the Gujarati trading communities, had the advantage of belonging to the economically most advanced region in India at the time, what is now Gujarat and Maharashtra. In addition, the Parsis had greater occupational mobility and fewer binding social commitments. Nevertheless, the most important reason for their success was their greater ability to adjust to British colonial rule and to develop a comprador and complementary relationship to British trading and shipping interests in Asia. Parsi businessmen loaned funds to the British, apprenticed their wards to English firms, and hired Europeans to take charge of their ships. In contrast to this, Hindus and Muslims, because of their involvement in earlier civil and military administration, were more likely to resist economic cooperation with the English.[15]

The Parsis[16] and Gujaratis were the dominant Indian entrepreneurs in Bombay's textile manufacturing, finance, and foreign trade; in Ahmedabad's textile industry after the middle of the nineteenth century; and in the small beginnings in Indian heavy industry early in the twentieth century.[17] Despite the unfavorable climate for textile mills and the location away from the port, Ahmedabad in Gujarat was one of the few major manufacturing cities to develop a class of industrial entrepreneurs indigenous to the region. Howard Spodek attributes this to the development of a suitable socioeconomic milieu for the rise of industrial entrepreneurship, with an emphasis on the development of social overhead capital, the improvement in political climate, the high business morality, the establishment of financial and management institutions, and the availability of many complementary factors.[18] Textile manufacturing in the leading southern center, Coimbatore, Tamil Nadu, was developed by two southern Indian groups, the Chettis, a money-lending community, and the Naidus, a local landowning class.

In the nineteenth century, the leading business communities in Calcutta and vicinity were Marwaris, while local Bengali trading *jati*s were virtually unrepresented. The lack of indigenous entrepreneurship in Bengal, a deficiency which extends to the present, stems in part from the discrimination and duplicity of the British in the nineteenth century and the low esteem placed on business occupations. In the early nineteenth century, participation of Bengalis in activities competitive with the British, such as international trade, resulted in the subsequent exclusion of Bengalis from modern business. In a number of cases in the 1880s, Bengali firms with established reputations were defrauded by British partners, an action that led many Bengali businessmen to retreat from trade and commerce. In addition, although Bengalis admired the boldness and daring of the ancient romantic merchant-prince and the modern industrialist, they placed a low value on the mundane pursuits of traditional businessmen such as the petty trader. The Bengali business classes, having spurned traditional business and being excluded from modern business, could find no middle ground suitable for their talents. This lack of participation in traditional business virtually precluded upward mobility to modern business.[19] Finally, the higher educational attainments of Bengalis as compared to Marwaris has offered the former a greater number of options to business.

In the nineteenth century, a large number of Marwaris emigrated to enter key entrepreneurial positions in trade and finance in Calcutta

and Bombay, in part because of the new economic roles (as inter-
mediaries, agents, financiers, and suppliers of armies) that British rule
provided. Many Marwaris were not only impelled by a series of bad
harvests to move to trade, but were also induced to emigrate by impediments to social mobility erected by the privileged *mut suddin*s (or
court merchants).[20]
    The business activities of the Marwaris in the nineteenth century
complemented British business pursuits. Once the Marwaris had
achieved a footing in the Bengali economy, they were able to rise
rapidly as a result of their hard work and commercial acumen, their
family solidarity conducive to mobilizing capital and entering entrepreneurial positions, and the fact that, as aliens, local business
values and sanctions did not inhibit them. Although the Marwaris,
subordinate to the British, did not begin to establish major manufacturing ventures until World War I, their control of a large part of the
indigenous banking system and ability to lend to other community
members facilitated their becoming the foremost Indian industrial
community in the last four decades or so.[21]

Present-Day Communities

Today the Marwaris, Parsis, and Gujarati trading *jati*s are the leading
Indian communities in modern industry and banking, especially in
major cities such as Bombay and Calcutta. Lamb and Timberg explain
the rise of these communities in large-scale manufacturing in terms of
factors such as control over several operating firms through the
managing agency, dominance of the indigenous banking system, community mobilization of resources, intra-community business linkages,
and intra-community marriage networks.[22]
    Since independence, refugee Hindu traders from Sindh (now part of
Pakistan) have become prominent in trade, real estate, and construction in some major cities. Similar to the pattern in a number of
business communities in earlier periods, they are now becoming industrialists, as illustrated by the case of A. R. Balchandani below.

EMPIRICAL STUDIES OF ENTREPRENEURSHIP AND SOCIAL COMMUNITY
The Punjab

Several studies investigate the relationship between *varna, jati,* and
social community, on the one hand, and entrepreneurship on the
other. Leighton W. Hazlehurst examines the effect of *jati,* socioeco-

nomic class, kinship structure, and social community in a Punjabi city of 50,000 on the social context in which entrepreneurship is undertaken. The analysis, based on observation and informal interview, encompasses entrepreneurial activity in all the major sectors of the city's economy—trade, manufacturing, and finance.[23]

The displacement of populations resulting from the partition of India had a major impact on the structure of entrepreneurship and class, especially in areas close to the India-Pakistan border with relatively large economic opportunities, such as Ram Nagar, a pseudonym for the city studied by Hazlehurst. The supply of trading entrepreneurs in the city was augmented substantially because a disproportionate share of refugees from West Pakistan were traders and administrative arrangements made it more likely for refugees to receive compensation for losses in urban areas.[24] A large majority of the displaced merchants who resettled in urban areas in eastern Punjab were Khatris or Aroras. Many of the subcaste distinctions among these groups have been obscured. One of the reasons for this is the disassociation from orthodox casteism which has resulted from religious reform movements (such as Sikhism and the Arya Samaj), where *jati* identity has become blurred. A second explanation is the high degree of occupational and spatial mobility leading to the erasing of old marriage networks among persons of similar status because of the scattering of possible marriage partners throughout the country. A final reason is the difficulty of assessing the validity of claims to status by refugees. Thus, it may be more accurate to think of the Khatris and Aroras in Ram Nagar as members of occupational groups rather than as members of endogamous *jati*s with well-defined caste rituals and behavior. Their social status within the city has been influenced primarily by local factors and is more ambiguous and less consistent among local groups than is usually the case.[25]

The arrival of displaced persons from West Pakistan helped weaken the dominant positions of the Aggarwal Banias, a Vaishya *jati,* in certain sectors of the economy such as trade. In addition, the relative economic position of the Banias declined for other reasons—the loss of Muslim tenants and debtors who fled to West Pakistan during the partition, and legislation passed to restrain entrepreneurs with substantial wealth. Since partition the Banias have united with the Suds, a lower caste, to control the city's timber business. They wanted to maintain the social status and economic power of the two major "local" business classes against the pressure of displaced persons.[26]

Hazelhurst notes that refugee entrepreneurs tend to be more innovative in business than local entrepreneurs, although he gives no reason.[27] I offer explanations for this in chapter 4.

West Bengal

Owens finds that in Howrah, a part of the Calcutta urban agglomeration, 65 percent of the entrepreneurs in small engineering units were Mahisyas, a cultivator caste, compared to 25 percent of the population of Howrah District. This is unusual, as agriculture is rarely mentioned as a background for industrial entrepreneurs in less-developed economies. However, the Mahisyas in the sample are best conceived of not as cultivators but as a subgroup which for several generations had been moving off the land and establishing ties with urban business and industry.[28] In addition, though not mentioned by Owens, the socioeconomic status and educational attainment of entrepreneurs in small-scale industries which require lengthy apprentice training are not likely to be high. As I point out in my study of Nigerian entrepreneurs, this may be due to the fact that the teenage boy with a high socioeconomic background who obtains a good formal education in preparation for a white-collar job usually foregoes the investment of time and money for low-status apprentice training.[29]

Tamil Nadu

Berna confines his empirical study, conducted in 1957, to manufacturing enterprises in light-engineering industry in Tamil Nadu with 50 to 250 persons employed. His findings are based on interviews with entrepreneurs of fifty-two firms and outside sources familiar with the firms. The sample is based on firms in Madras City and Coimbatore and their vicinities listed in the Madras State Factory List for 1956.[30]

Berna contends that traditional occupation and *jati* have very little impact in determining entry into entrepreneurial endeavors. The fifty-two entrepreneurs are members of ten different social communities, although forty-one of the fifty-two are from three communities—the Naidu, a land-owning class from the warrior *varna*; the Brahmin; and the Chettiar, a southern Indian trading community. Only four of the sample entrepreneurs are in direct line with the traditional caste-assigned family occupation.[31] This break with the traditional occupation indicates to Berna that in explaining entrepreneurial activity "sociological factors, such as caste, attachment to traditional activities, and approval or disapproval of the social group to which a potential entrepreneur belongs are less important than economic factors such as access to capital and possession of business experience and technical knowledge."[32]

Hoselitz argues, however, that if Berna's sample is characteristic of Tamil Nadu industrial entrepreneurs in general, the social structure of the state must be undergoing a profound change. One important indication of this change is the decline in occupational choices assigned by caste. He indicates that sociological explanations are needed for these departures from traditional occupations. Brahmins, for example, have recently been more inclined to become entrepreneurs than previously for a number of reasons: discrimination encountered in universities and government as a reaction against their favored social position in the colonial period, the decline in the number of caste-determined occupations available, an increase in status of business occupations resulting from sociopolitical emphasis on the need for economic growth, and the wealth and influence available for investment in training and new enterprises. In short, with socioeconomic change leading to the erosion of the Brahmins' traditional position and the present emphasis on economic development, they were led to see entrepreneurship as increasingly attractive.[33] A parallel exists in Nigeria, where a large number of Yoruba and Hausa traditional political rulers thwarted possible socioeconomic decline accompanying modernization by using their wealth and influence to establish sizeable trading and manufacturing firms.[34]

In concluding that sociological factors are less important than economic factors, Berna has raised some important questions. Hoselitz's challenge to Berna's conclusion, together with the prior Papanek-Hagen controversy,[35] has helped clarify some of these issues. What the controversies do indicate is the limitations of the approach of a single discipline to a discussion of the determinants of entrepreneurship. For example, in the case of the Brahmins, impelled by both their declining socioeconomic position and advantages accruing from their residual wealth and influence (access to capital, good educational background), entrepreneurial activity resulted from the interaction of both social and economic factors.

Berna found that the largest group of entrepreneurs (twelve of fifty-two), when classified according to immediate vocational background, was graduate engineers.[36] Although he finds this difficult to explain, it is perhaps not so surprising in light of the relatively large output of engineers and their relatively low average salary and high rate of unemployment in the post–World-War-II period. One notices, for example, that few industrial entrepreneurial positions are filled by ex-civil servants, who as a group have relatively high salaries, good working conditions, attractive fringe benefits, and secure tenure. To explain entrepreneurial participation among groups such as graduate engineers and civil servants, it is useful to consider the alternative remuneration available, an approach used here.

One point needs to be considered when generalizing on the basis of the Berna study. Recruitment to new occupations which are created through industrialization and are not in the caste hierarchy is more likely to be open to a wide variety of *jatis*.

Singer's analysis of information received from interviews of Madras City industrial leaders in 1964 serves as a basis for challenging Max Weber's contention[37] that the caste system, concept of ritual purity, and the doctrines of fate (karma), duty (dharma), and rebirth associated with Hinduism are not conducive to the economic development of India. According to Singer, Weber's error in examining Indian religion was to rely on scriptural texts to construct the ideal-typical Hindu, a mistake Weber did not make in his investigation of ascetic Protestantism in the West.[38] Caste affiliation and religious beliefs are found by Singer to be less decisive than factors such as individual and family experience, previous occupation, education, and capital as determinants of recruitment to and success in positions of industrial leadership. Paralleling critiques of Weber's linking the Protestant ethic with the spirit of capitalism,[39] Singer places more emphasis upon the rational adaptability of Hinduism to innovation, modernization, and industrialization, and less on the intrinsic affinity of the Hindu value system to industrial capitalism. Ironically, his evidence indicates that Hindu industrialists, as Weber's Puritan entrepreneurs, exhibited "worldly" asceticism in economic activity, sensed a "calling" to responsibility in a secular vocation, and believed that prosperity was a sign of divine blessing.[40]

ENTREPRENEURSHIP AND THE CASTE SYSTEM

Many observers contend that the caste system and its series of obligations (which reinforce the practice of following a family occupation) tend to reduce occupational mobility, technical change, and innovation, which are considered to be objectionable and ritually dangerous.[41] As Hoselitz states it, industrial "entrepreneurship can develop only in a society in which cultural norms permit variability in the choice of paths of life in which the relevant processes of socialization of the individual are not so completely standardized and demanding conformity to a prescribed pattern that the bases for appropriate personality development leading to productive orientation are absent."[42] In a society which emphasizes that each person has a duty (dharma) appropriate to his station in life—a duty which depends upon the caste into which he is born[43]—very little variability would seem to be possible.

However, Baldwin points out that in "Indian industry, the caste system seemed to be considerably looser and more flexible than it often appears to outsiders at first glance. Its novelty, quaintness, and historical importance produce an exaggerated estimate of its present role in the cities, where disintegration may proceed rapidly."[44] Despite the powerful socioreligious sanctions given the caste system, there are several dynamic factors making fluidity and flexibility in occupational and caste structures possible.

In the first place, caste ranking in any given area is not defined precisely because of the substantial inconsistencies in the stratified interactions among individuals of different castes in the numerous ritual, political, and economic spheres. The fact that interactions which establish caste precedence most firmly are so disparately organized around the activities of many self-directing households and lineage groups favors a diversity in individual opinions concerning caste rankings. This diversity results in greater potential mobility for individual *jatis*.[45]

Discrepancies between the ritual rank and economic standing of a *jati* can stimulate mobility. A wealthy *jati* can use the power of its members as landlords, employers, financiers, and patrons to prevent other castes from blocking its adoption of the rituals and symbols of higher *jatis* and its claim to a higher position in the caste hierarchy. In a village in Uttar Pradesh studied by McKim Marriott, the Baghele Goatherds became the dominant landholders and creditors after they had purchased substantial plots of land from an insolvent high-caste landlord in the 1930s. With their new wealth, the Goatherds were able to acquire a higher position in the exchanges of food and in other ritual interactions which help to establish caste ranking. For example, leading Goatherd families were able to persuade less-affluent higher-caste individuals (including the most impecunious Brahmins) to accept food, and to induce indigent members of their own *jati* to refuse foods from castes of near-equal status.[46] In some cases dominant castes have used physical violence and economic boycott to prevent lower *jatis* from adopting the symbols of higher castes.[47] However, the Goat-herds had enough economic and political power that the dominant castes had few reciprocal penalties available to prevent their adoption of high caste symbols, and their concomitant upward mobility.[48]

Second, the caste system is capable of making certain accommodations to changes in the composition of demand for occupations resulting from technical change and economic structural change. Families in *jatis* with shortages may adopt young males from *jatis* with surpluses. In some cases, persons may not be constrained by the occupational duties of the caste, even though they may be expected to fulfill the ritual obligations of the caste occupation. Also, it is possible for the occupational duties of the caste to be modified over time, as in the case of the low-caste Leatherworkers in the Uttar Pradesh village who changed their occupation to that of middle-caste Weavers. In addition, religious injunctions are flexible enough and the inducements of the modern industrial system powerful enough so that caste and religious taboos and sanctions can change.[49] A further point is that certain nontraditional occupations such as modern industry, government service, and day labor can recruit from all classes. And in certain circles in the big cities, there are a number of rich, well-educated, Westernized persons who ignore *jati* regulations and whose occupations bear no relation to the traditional occupation of the *jati* into which they were born.[50]

Third, migration such as that by displaced persons during the India-Pakistan partition tends to obscure old marriage networks necessary to preserve the endogamy of *jatis*. In addition, the status claims of immigrant groups may be difficult to appraise. Also, immigrants are less likely to be bound by the restrictive sanctions of the local community and more likely to be stimulated by the tradition-breaking forces of a new environment.[51]

In the fourth place, the rise of new religious sects or reform groups frequently may erase some of the old caste distinctions, as in the case of the Sikhs and Arya Samaj.[52] However, in some cases converts find that their *jati* identification is carried with them to their new sect.[53] In addition, socioreligious groups, such as the Parsis, with no established or defined position in the social structure, may have more flexibility in moving to new and nontraditional forms of occupations.[54]

At this point, it is useful to discuss Hazlehurst's distinction between the cultural and structural dimensions of caste. Entrepreneurs "participate in numerous cross-cutting social relationships and pursue diverse economic interests while still maintaining the cultural boundaries of caste."[55] In some cases, the ritual ranking of a caste may be relatively rigid, whereas its socioeconomic ranking may be flexible. Indeed, it is possible that individuals and subgroups within the *jati* may be relatively mobile in socioeconomic status and power. Moreover, structural changes arising from development may lead to realignments of castes. New intercaste cooperation can result in changes in social status and economic power of groups.[56] Finally, the status of *jati* and occupational groups is frequently a local matter. Caste ranking— especially socioeconomic ranking—is not completely ascribed but is based in part upon the power and achievement of the group.

Since India has been a parliamentary democracy where strength depends more on numbers than on caste ranking, castes have been able to rise by procuring favorable government legislation and policy. Castes successful in being labeled "backward" have been given financial assistance or relatively high quotas in educational institutions and government positions. In addition, certain occupational groups with a high priority in the economic plan have been assisted, whereas certain occupational groups thought to be retarding socioeconomic development have been restrained.[57]

Studies available indicate that despite the impediments to mobility resulting from the caste system, it does have some elements of flexibility which make it possible for the system to adapt to aggregate and structural economic change. However, more research is needed on the dynamic elements affecting the caste system and occupational structure.

ENTREPRENEURSHIP AND THE FAMILY

For a large proportion of firms in India, the basic unit of entrepreneurship is the extended family. India's industrialists, for example, are usually members of old trading families, which in the past frequently exercised control of a number of firms through the managing agency firm. This is discussed below. Many prominent Indian business families are involved in several companies, which in some cases represent complementary interests. Frequently, there is specialization by family members according to industrial activity, geographical division, or management function.[58] The advantages of a family-controlled business are its ability to mobilize large amounts of resources, its quick unified decision making, and its access to trustworthy personnel to oversee operations.[59] The disadvantages are that the business may not obtain the most talented persons for positions within the firm.

Few data are available on the general impact of the Indian extended family on entrepreneurial activity. However, the Indian case might be expected to be similar to the Nigerian case, where one study indicates that the extended family, with its ability to mobilize large resources, facilitates the acquisition of entrepreneurial training and the establishment of firms. On the other hand, like the Nigerian case, the joint family in India would be likely to hinder the expansion of firms by diverting resources for current consumption which might otherwise have been reinvested in the business.[60] Although I touch on this below, more research is necessary to assess the relative significance of the positive and negative effects of the Indian extended family on entrepreneurial activity.

Auspicious marriages for children in business families are generally considered important for both social and economic reasons. Of course, in most parts of Hindu society, marriage arrangements though based on clan exogamy, are based on caste endogamy so that the purity of the group or caste is maintained. An individual's status depends upon the maintenance of endogamy within the *jati* or subgroup.[61] However, for the business family more may be required of the marriage than just *jati* endogamy.

For the Bania business community, as for many other communities in Ram Nagar the marriage ceremony has economic as well as ritual significance. Business savings are often used for marriage expenditures, which are generally well calculated to lead to advantageous interrelationships. Access to credit and avenues for mobility are dependent upon the complex network of relationships arising from marriage. Marriage ceremonies and the payments of dowry serve as public statements to the local community—especially local creditors—of one's financial position and are observed closely. Nonkinsmen who have economic interactions with the family are concerned about the family's total lineage and marriage network. A major offense, such as the marriage of a daughter into a lower *jati*, can result in the family being outcast from the Banias and leads to the prohibition of economic relationships, business partnerships, and marriage partnerships in the community. On the other hand, the respect and prestige deriving from an auspicious marriage may be important in improving the status of the family and setting the course for future business transactions and endeavors.[62]

In much of village India, a person is granted credit as a member of a particular *jati* or family, rather than as an individual. Frequently, the creditor-debtor relationship has a social significance beyond the economic relationship. The relationship between creditor and debtor takes on a *"jajmani-*like" character or semipermanent patron-client relationship, in which the creditor provides virtually unconditional access to credit for goods and services for the customer in return for the customer's continuous loyalty and patronage.[63]

To summarize, in many cases the extended family is the unit of entrepreneurship, supplying managerial and financial resources needed for business operations. The fact that the extended family may also be the basic consumption unit means that resources may frequently be diverted from business investment to support family members with little or no earnings. Finally, the interrelationships provided by the marriage networks of the family can help determine the access to credit and opportunities for mobility by family members in entrepreneurial endeavors.

THE MANAGING AGENCY SYSTEM

Because of the important legacy of the managing agency system, a system unique to India, I shall discuss the system and the way it affected the organization and context of entrepreneurial endeavors. The institution, which originated in the first half of the nineteenth century[64] and was abolished in 1970, was the dominant type of organization for the joint stock company, the prevailing form of enterprise among firms with over 250 persons employed.[65]

In the managing agency system—a system which especially pervaded modern industry, trade, and agriculture—the administration, finance, and promotion of one or more legally separate companies were controlled by a single firm.[66] The distinguishing feature of the system was the contractual agreement between the managing agents and the board of directors of the operating company, in which the agents received commissions and fees for providing management over a specified period of time, usually twenty years or longer. In practice, the managing agents usually undertook entrepreneurial responsibility beyond the routine management function.[67] The managing agency firm, which frequently controlled more than one operating enterprise, often in the same or related industry, generally could be thought of as the basic entrepreneurial unit.[68]

The managing firm was originally developed so that English managers could be utilized more extensively and so that owners who returned to Britain could place their business in the hands of "reputable agents." The managing agency of a reputable managing firm put its credit and holdings as a whole behind the enterprise being managed.[69] The indigenous managing agency, on the other hand, was an extension of relationships in an older family firm. Most of the members of the agency were relatives or at least members of the same caste.[70] Generally, the managing agents and their friends comprised the board of directors of the operating company that contracted with the managing agency firm.[71]

The major advantages of the managing agency system were the economies of large-scale organization—economies in production, marketing, management, financial services, and vertical linkages.[72] The system especially helped to conserve scarce entrepreneurial talent and to mobilize venture capital. Entrepreneurial skills could be utilized more effectively because of specialization and economies of scale in entrepreneurial endeavor.[73] A small group of businessmen could concentrate their capital in a new operating firm, arrange a contract between the firm and a managing agency, attract capital from other sources as the operating firm became established, withdraw capital from the firm while retaining control through the managing agency firm, and begin the process again in a new operating firm.[74]

One of the disadvantages of the system was that it increased the concentration of economic power within and across industries. Even in years prior to 1970, there was a shift on the part of new companies away from the managing agency system to more direct forms of management as a result of the attempt by government to discourage economic concentration by increasing competition from the public sector and tightening regulation of the agencies.[75] A further disadvantage of the system was that it hampered the development of new entrepreneurial and managerial skills, especially among the indigenous population, which required "learning by doing."

Despite the argument by Joseph Schumpeter that economic concentration may be associated with internal economies of scale and technological innovation,[76] I consider the abolition of the managing agency system to be desirable. Prima facie evidence would seem to indicate that a large number of managing agency firms reached a level of output well beyond the realization of internal economies of scale. The fact that the managing agency system was frequently being used to acquire control of well-established businesses, to operate several enterprises in one industry, and to increase the concentration of wealth in a few families[77] would indicate that further encouragement of the system would have been inconsistent with the objectives of the state to decrease economic inequalities and increase efficiency of resource allocation.

ACHIEVEMENT MOTIVATION TRAINING AND ENTREPRENEURSHIP

In recent years, an increasing number of industrial extension centers in India have introduced achievement motivation training as a major part of their programs to develop entrepreneurs. The intellectual catalyst for this training has been the writings of McClelland and his associates—especially the findings in a path-breaking experiment in India.[78] The primary focus of this section is an evaluation of the efforts of the McClelland group to use achievement motivation training in the development of Indian entrepreneurs.

The evidence is strong that a person learns unconsciously in his early childhood the patterns of behavior that are safest and most rewarding, and that this learning substantially influences his adult behavior. For example, the individual who is expected and encouraged to be curious, creative, and independent as a child is more likely to engage in innovative and entrepreneurial activity as an adult. Although a society might consciously attempt to nurture imagination, self-reliance, and achievement orientation in the socialization and education of children, this process has been considered by scholars to be at best slow and uncertain, and to take at least a generation before deliberative efforts at improvement affect entrepreneurial and innovative activity and economic growth.[79]

McClelland, in *The Achieving Society*, contends that a society with a generally high need for achievement or "urge to improve" (n Ach) produces more energetic entrepreneurs who, in turn, bring about more rapid economic development. As a first step, he establishes a significant positive relationship between n Ach scores (in children's readers) and subsequent rates of growth in electrical output (a proxy for economic growth) in a cross-national sample from the twentieth century. Then McClelland finds that those persons with a high n Ach are more likely to behave like an entrepreneur, i.e., (1) take personal responsibility for decisions; (2) prefer decisions involving a moderate degree of risk; and (3) evince interest in concrete knowledge of the results of decisions. Furthermore, his empirical evidence suggests that persons with high n Ach tend to be attracted into entrepreneurial positions (when society places a high prestige upon these occupations).[80]

The Achieving Society is pessimistic about the possibility of policy measures to induce substantial increases in n Ach, as this is dependent upon child-rearing techniques and parental attitudes. But even if these could be changed, it would be a long wait until the children grew up to have an impact upon entrepreneurial activity and economic growth. A logical next step for McClelland was to restate his theory to test whether n Ach might be increased among adults to enhance development.[81] Some might not include McClelland and Winter's work in a survey of works on Indian entrepreneurship, as the book is virtually devoid of a discussion of entrepreneurs and their motivation in terms of the Indian historical and sociocultural context.[82] Nevertheless, because of the importance of the pioneering studies of McClelland, the widespread use of achievement motivation training in programs to engender entrepreneurs and managers in poor countries, and the controversy over their use, a review of this work is essential.

His laboratory for this "intervention effort"[83] was southern and central India. Businessmen from Kakinada and Rajahmundry, Andhra Pradesh, and Vellore, Tamil Nadu, travelled to Hyderabad, Andhra Pradesh, in 1964–65 to take a ten-day course at the Small Industries Extension Training Institute, an institute of the Government of India which collaborated in the undertaking. The purpose of the experiment was to investigate whether achievement motivation could be inculcated in businessmen through motivational training courses in small groups, and whether the training would result in heightened business activity. In the course, students were to acquire a higher need to achieve through (1) learning to recognize and produce achievement-related fantasies; (2) self-study to ascertain how the achievement syndrome relates to their lives, careers, goals, and values; (3) attempting to define more precisely their basic goals, the blocks to these, methods to overcome blocks, and ways to measure progress toward these goals; and (4) the development of new interpersonal supports and reference groups to reinforce values associated with the urge to improve.[84]

I would argue that a program of n Ach acquisition for entrepreneurs, while it may very well be suitable to Western societies, is less likely to be appropriate in India. First, in a society with substantial limitations on resource availability, high n Ach, associated with a competitive spirit, "becomes a sin against one's fellows." When available resources are scarce, persons with a high need for cooperation will produce more than those with high n Ach.[85] Second, high n Ach may be appropriate where an individual can control his activity, but not where he faces substantial restraints on decision making.[86] Persons with a high n Ach may be frustrated and counterproductive in a large number of sectors of a society which places an emphasis on "a socialist pattern of society" with public and bureaucratic economic decision making. Third, a "course [which] is basically one of self-development" and which emphasizes "a personal decision" with regard to life goals[87] may have merit in the United States, where independence and self-reliance are emphasized, but not in India where the communal and family nexus are important in choices. In India, where the extended family is the basic unit for individual identification and orientation, and frequently for business ventures, n Ach, a measure of individual achievement motivation, does not explain entrepreneurial behavior.[88]

The authors seem not to be seriously aware of the moral ambiguities which arise when "change agents" primarily from an alien culture embark on "personality change" and behavior modification in a society which, by their own admission, they understand little.[89] Ashis Nandy puts it this way:

One must . . . recognize that something more than mere achievement training was involved. What these quasi-therapeutic interventions tried to do could be crudely summed up as an attempt to generate personality vectors functional to modern economic behavior and help individuals to integrate these vectors in their personality system by altering, among other things, self-image, significant others, access to the relevant aspects of their own fantasy life, and sense of efficacy vis-à-vis the external world. The inputs package represented, in this sense, more nearly a program of total personality change. Such a program of intervention demands some awareness of the cultural forces which shape a person's behaviour and with which he has to cope at so many levels as well as sectors of social living.[90]

One problem in interpreting the authors' findings is the lack of a genuine control group to compare with those entrepreneurs given the achievement motivation course. Given the claims of the course, the prestige of sponsorship by a Harvard Center, and the support of the District Collector, Chamber of Commerce, and leading local officials (e.g., in Kakinada),[91] it would not be surprising if the course had attracted a select group of entrepreneurs, especially interested in personal and business development. Among other things, the high level of personal capital and subsequent business activity of participants from Kakinada in the first two courses, in comparison to the last two courses, would suggest that the attempt, especially in early courses, to attract leading businessmen with a substantial interest in self-improvement, was successful.[92] A group of businessmen who did not participate in the course is labeled "Kakinada controls" by the authors. However, this group is not really a control group, because they could have taken the course, but did not. Neither is the group of businessmen from another coastal Andhra city, Rajahmundry, who never had the opportunity to sign up for the course a "control group." To obtain a bona fide control group—that is to control for the variable of desire to seek self and business improvement—it would have been essential to prevent some who sought to enroll in the course (perhaps a systematically paired control group) from taking the course.[93]

There is no information presented on the relationship between n Ach and entrepreneurial activity prior to training. Naturally, n Ach scores for participants increased after training, since they were guided in practice sessions to obtain higher scores than they did at first.[94] Otherwise, the only data available on n Ach scores is a comparison between participants who were active in expanding their business and those who were inactive. "For all practical purposes the n Ach acquisition and retention [scores for those active and those inactive] are identical."[95] On the other hand, other variables measured—the number of mutual friendship bonds with other participants, scores with regard to efficacy of thinking, and observations by the chief architect of the course regarding the probability of change by various participants—proved to be more powerful in predicting business activity than n Ach.[96]

The authors contend that the courses, as intended, had a number of benefits besides raising the participants' n Ach. Yet they present no hypothesis on the relationship between n Ach, economic opportunities, and social structure, and between these variables and entrepreneurial activity. Nandy contends that the authors' approach "still is not a comprehensive theory of personality which considers personality as an open system and individual motive structure as an interface between personal and community pasts."[97]

How does the performance of the course participants compare to what the authors considered a control group? Given the fact that the data on firm performance—employment, investment, sales, and so forth—over a five-year period were oral, and "given the continuous and apparently successful attempts to generate a "Hawthorne effect" (which also tends to obscure any personality change), there is a strong presumptive bias favoring positive results for the training."[98] Toward the end of the course, the faculty, through its help in preparing businessmen for future contacts and surveys by the sponsors, may have inadvertently reinforced a positive bias. Course participants were told that the staff of the host institute "would keep in touch with them not only informally over [the two-year] time period but would be back every six months to find out how they were doing in terms of their personal and group plan and in terms of such general business criteria as gross income, capital invested, profit, etc. They practiced filling out the forms they would be asked to return in six months' time so that they would be guided in their actions by the thoughts of how they would be evaluated later."[99] Reports from visitors who evaluated the entrepreneurs after the course suggest embarrassment by some respondents as a result of the lack of business progress, and "an occasional guilt feeling."[100] In view of this, it would not be surprising if the entrepreneurs overstated their progress, or understated their setbacks.

Yet despite the predilection for favorable reports on growth and performance, there are no significant differential percentage increases in gross incomes by the course participants, although there are significant differential percentage increases in the entrepreneur's time input, attempts to start new businesses, labor employed, and capital invested, when compared to those considered controls.[101] "Thus, if the test were to be treated as valid, it would indicate that motivational training engenders a willingness to increase inputs while at the same time it reduces entrepreneurial efficiency and, thereby, the returns to entrepreneurial effort."[102]

There is an alternative hypothesis to explain the association between n Ach and entrepreneurship. McClelland's data indicate that in the United States there is a positive correlation between social class and n Ach (p < .001). Black Americans, particularly those from the lower classes, score especially low in n Ach.[103] Robert A. LeVine's study of achievement motivation in Nigeria indicates a significant positive correlation between n Ach, on the one hand, and paternal class and education, on the other.[104] However, because McClelland and LeVine's conceptual matrix is not oriented to deal with class analysis, they do not pursue the implications of these findings. Upperclass individuals, who encounter fewer blocks (i.e., deficiencies in education, training, experience, and skills, and lack of capital and contacts), are more likely to be achievement oriented, and to be able to take advantage of entrepreneurial and other economic opportunities. On the other hand, for those members of underprivileged classes who live in a "subculture of poverty," low n Ach and low aspirations are an adaptation to the low probability of economic success resulting from blocks to economic advancement in society, educational institutions, and the family milieu.[105] McClelland and Winter are correct when they contend that "energetic striving to improve one's lot may seem rational enough to a man with high *n* Achievement, but not to a man with low *n* Achievement." But whereas the lack of striving by those with low n Ach is a result of a lack of sensitivity to changes in economic opportunities and incentives in their scheme,[106] it is a result of blocks to class mobility in the alternative scheme.

My hypothesis is that n Ach is not a primary variable, but merely a correlate of socioeconomic class, which is significantly related to entrepreneurial activity through differential provision of economic opportunity. The basis for this hypothesis is not only the positive correlation between class and n Ach discussed in the preceding paragraph, but also the positive relationships I find between socioeconomic class and entrepreneurship in my study and my interpretation of other studies cited below. To be more specific, a highly disproportional number of the industrial entrepreneurs (especially successful ones) in my Vizag sample are from high castes and from families with a high economic status. Furthermore, I argue that an analysis of other empirical studies undertaken in India, Pakistan, the Philippines, Nigeria, Greece, and the United States indicates that the socioeconomic class of entrepreneurs is high.

Unfortunately, McClelland and Winter have no data on the relationship between caste or class, on the one hand, and n Ach, on the other,[107] and I have access to no other information on this relationship among Indian entrepreneurs. Thus, one can only suggest by inference that all cross-relationships between n Ach, socioeconomic class, and entrepreneurial activity are positive. In the future, scholars might wish to investigate more explicitly the relationship between n Ach and socioeconomic class in samples of entrepreneurs.

Whatever the difference between the McClelland approach and my alternative approach in terms of explanatory variables, there is an equally important implication in terms of the legitimacy of the position of the dominant elites in society. For example, McClelland and Winter indicate that in Pennsylvania, unemployed workers with high n Ach were more likely to seek and find jobs than those with low n Ach, although a critic might suggest that those most unemployable adapt to this state by keeping their achievement expectations low. The McClelland paradigm, with its premise that n Ach can be changed, suggests that the individual bears responsibility for unemployment or for lack of entrepreneurial activity. The alternative approach implies that the fault may lie, in part, with the impediments that society and its dominant classes place in the road to upward mobility to high-level jobs and business activity. One issue, which I elaborate on in subsequent chapters, is the extent to which the economically weak are responsible for poverty, unemployment, and a lack of entrepreneurial activity, and the extent to which their class mobility is impeded by the cumulative advantages of the prevailing economic elite.

Since 1971, there have been several efforts by Indian institutions to include achievement motivation training in programs for entrepreneurs. In contrast to the projects undertaken by McClelland and his associates, these programs have been initiated, planned, and directed by indigenous personnel.

In early 1970, the Gujarat Industrial Investment Corporation, the Gujarat Development Corporation, and the Gujarat Financial Corporation jointly established an entrepreneurship development program. In 1971, achievement motivation training was added to an existing program which included practical training in management, marketing and finance, assistance in project conception and planning, and field trips to view business firms.[108] Recently the Maharashtra Small Scale Industries Development Corporation (MSSIDC) has used the techniques of motivation training, together with management training, to try to assist in the development of industrial entrepreneurs. Finally, in June 1975, the National Institute of Motivational and Institutional Development (NIMID) was formed in Bombay and Poona to promote and support research, training, and consultancy in motivational change; entrepreneurial activity; technological diffusion; and institutional development, especially in economically backward areas.[109] It is too early to evaluate the effectiveness of the achievement motivation training programs of the MSSIDC or NIMID.

There has not been a full evaluation of the effectiveness of the program to train entrepreneurs in Gujarat.[110] Even less is available to assess the contribution of only one component part of the program, such as achievement motivation training. However, a few comments about the Gujarat scheme may be appropriate. Buchele maintains that the Gujarat program was "[p]robably the most successful entrepreneur development program in India" even prior to the use of achievement motivation training.[111] Yet administrators and trainees are convinced that the addition of motivational training has been useful.[112]

At this point, I would suspend judgment on the efficacy of motivation training in Gujarat until further evidence is available. Nevertheless, there are reasons why these motivation training programs, run entirely by indigenous personnel, might be more effective and less objectionable than those conducted by the McClelland group. First, it is possible that indigenous "change agents," in contrast to foreigners, can more readily adapt the training to the needs and aspirations of prospective local entrepreneurs, while avoiding some of the unnecessary violations of local cultural norms and social mores. One obvious advantage of indigenization is the wider option in the use of language; usually, the use of the regional language instead of English increases the number of candidates who can potentially benefit from the course. In the second place, it is easier for indigenous personnel to establish programs to try to attract entrepreneurs from underprivileged groups. For example, the MSSIDC charged concessional entrance fees to candidates from underprivileged classes (i.e., "scheduled castes, scheduled tribes and other backward communities").[113]

Third, it may be that achievement motivation training is effective only as a part of an integrated package of training, which includes training in management, finance, and marketing, parts of the programs of the NIMID, and the Gujarat and Maharashtra industrial corporations.[114] Perhaps an accentuation of the achievement motivation is likely to be eventually frustrated unless there is some concomitant business training to help entrepreneurs cope with potential new or expanded business activity. However, the sparsity of empirical evidence on the topic makes future research essential in order to determine whether the indigenous efforts at achievement motivation training in India have been effective.

CONCLUSION

This chapter supplies certain perspectives on the history of entrepreneurial activity, caste and communal composition of businessmen, the relationship of government to private business, and the organization of entrepreneurial activity that cannot be provided on the basis of a single empirical study. The information in this chapter, by encompassing a wide range of studies on various regions in India, provides a backdrop for the investigation of entrepreneurial activity in Visakhapatnam, Andhra Pradesh.

There are a number of gaps in the literature on Indian entrepreneurship. Part of the contribution of this study is to address itself to two questions generally lacking in previous empirical work. What are the differences in opportunites for entrepreneurial activity between the privileged and underprivileged portions of the population? What are the factors related to the success of entrepreneurs?

The studies in this survey lack statistical data to compare the caste and class composition of entrepreneurs to that of the population. The official census and sample surveys do not acquire aggregate data on caste. However, since information is available from the Ramana study on caste composition in Vizag, this study can indicate the extent to which various castes are overrepresented and underrepresented in entrepreneurial activity, and, as a comparison, blue-collar work. I try to explain the differential participation in entrepreneurial activity by caste on the basis of its correlation with education, income, economic class, occupational status, and work experience.

Except for Singh's analysis at a high level of aggregation and Berna's study of factors related to the growth in the resources of production hired by firms, there have been no systematic studies of determinants of entrepreneurial success. In large part, the reason for this lack is that none of the studies on entrepreneurship utilizes measures of entrepreneurial and firm success. The lack of these measures is only partly because of the difficulty of obtaining access to firm records. Usually data are at least available on output or value added, so that it can be related to other variables. For example, Berna had access to data on output which were not utilized.[115] Although Berna does discuss firm growth, it is the growth of inputs, capital, and labor. This growth is no measure of firm performance unless one assumes fixed input-output coefficients, in which case entrepreneurship has no effect upon output.

4

SOCIOECONOMIC ORIGINS

"Unto every one which hath shall be given; and from him that hath not, even that he hath shall be taken away from him."

Luke 19:26 (The Bible, King James Version)

ALTHOUGH several empirical studies have investigated the socioeconomic origins of entrepreneurs in parts of India, these studies lack the data essential for comparing the origins of entrepreneurs with that of the population as a whole, and for relating socioeconomic characteristics of the entrepreneurs to their success. In this chapter, data on the distribution of entrepreneurs by class (paternal economic status) and caste are compared with information on the population at large, and are related to the educational attainment, entrepreneurial and managerial experience, initial capital, access to government assistance, and business success of the entrepreneurs. The evidence here provides a test of the prevailing view in the literature that industrial entrepreneurship is a vehicle for upward mobility to success in business.

A period of rapid industrial growth and economic modernization, as in India's independence era, does not remove the advantages of ascribed status, even in entrepreneurial activity in manufacturing. The traditional Indian upper classes—local rulers and administrators, landlords, and Brahmins—whose strength is a legacy of the feudal and colonial periods, have allied, and in some cases overlapped, with the capitalist, political, and bureaucratic elites, most of whom originated from high-income families, to control much of the access to key business positions. Families and communities with wealth and position use the monopoly advantage resulting from ready access to capital, greater information and mobility, superior education and training, privileged access to licenses and concessions from government, and the luxury of a longer planning horizon, to become industrial entrepreneurs in disproportionate numbers.

THE CONCEPT OF CASTE

By influencing the responsiveness of persons to economic incentives and the extent of experiences, resources, and connections appropriate for business activity, sociocultural variables affect the position and elasticity of the supply of entrepreneurship and the success of the entrepreneurs. As argued in the previous chapter, entrepreneurs are classified by *varna* (Brahmin, Kshatriya, Vaishya, Sudra, Harijan, and various non-Hindu religious communities), even though Sudras designated themselves by *jati*. Furthermore, the sample is too small to make generalizations about *jati*s. In addition, the *varna* ranking of a caste aids in defining and identifying a person socially. Although *varna* may include a number of *jati*s, it is highly correlated with parental economic status and class in Vizag,[1] as well as India in general, and can, with other indicators of these rankings, help in analyzing social mobility. Despite the diversity of the Sudras, in the aggregate they correspond to the middle socioeconomic group between twice-born castes and Harijans.

CASTE, FAMILY, AND SOCIAL COMMUNITY

Data on the caste composition of the sample and city indicate that high Hindu castes, Muslims, and Sikhs were overrepresented among the entrepreneurs. Fifty-two percent of the entrepreneurs (in contrast to only 11 percent of blue-collar workers) were from twice-born Hindu castes which comprise only 26 percent of the population of Vizag city. The Sudras, who comprise 57 percent of the population of the city account for only 28 percent of the entrepreneurs.[2] None of the entrepreneurs, but a disproportionate share of blue-collar workers, was from low-caste backgrounds (i.e., Harijans and Protestant or Roman Catholic Christians) (table 1).[3] There was a significant positive relationship between the caste ranking of the Hindu population and representation in entrepreneurial activity (table 2). The relationship is still significant even if the dominant business community, the Vaishyas, are eliminated (table 3), and even if the analysis is confined to entrepreneurs born in Andhra Pradesh (table 4).

TABLE 1
Caste Origin and Birthplace of Entrepreneurs

Caste	Number of Entrepreneurs born in A.P.[a]	Number of Entrepreneurs born outside A.P.[a]	Number of Entrepreneurs (Total)	Percentage of Entrepreneurs (Total)	Percentage of Blue-Collar Workers in Vizag[b]	Percentage of Population of Vizag[c]
Brahmin	9	2	11	20.36	2.22	21.45
Kshatriya	5	0	5	9.26	8.89	2.35
Vaishya	4	8	12	22.22	0.00	2.15
Sudra	14	1	15	27.78	57.78	56.86
Harijan	0	0	0	0.00	15.56	11.25
Muslim	4	3	7	12.96	6.67	1.30
Christian (Protestant, Catholic)	0	0	0	0.00	8.89	4.55
Christian (Syrian)	0	1	1	1.85	0.00	0.00[d]
Sikh	0	2	2	3.70	0.00	0.00[d]
Parsi	0	1	1	1.85	0.00	0.00[d]
Unknown	0	0	0	0.00	0.00	0.10
TOTAL	36	18	54	99.98[e]	100.01[e]	100.00

a. Andhra Pradesh.
b. Ramana, "Caste and Society," p. 137.
c. Ibid., p. 29.
d. None of the three groups is represented in the Ramana sample. Sikhs make up 0.09 percent and Parsis 0.01 percent of the population of Vizag City, according to the 1961 census. Syrian Christians are not separated from Protestant and Roman Catholic Christians in the census, but Ramana suggests that less than 1 percent of the Christians (i.e., less than 0.05 percent of the total population) are Syrian.
e. May not add up to 100.00 because of rounding.

TABLE 2
Frequency Distribution of Hindu Entrepreneurs by Caste Ranking

Caste Ranking	Observed Frequency[a]	Expected Frequency[b]
Twice-born castes	28	11.9
Middle and low castes	15	31.1

NOTES: Sudras and Harijans comprise the middle and low castes.
Calculated value of $\chi^2 = 30.11$, χ^2 at the .01 level of significance with 1 d.f. = 6.64.
a. Based on the third column in table 1.
b. Based on the share of each caste grouping in the Hindu population of Vizag, as computed from the last column in table 1.

TABLE 3
Frequency Distribution of Non-Vaishya Hindu Entrepreneurs by Caste Ranking

Caste Ranking	Observed Frequency[a]	Expected Frequency[b]
Twice-born castes	16	8.0
Middle and low castes	15	23.0

NOTES: Brahmins and Kshatriyas comprise the twice-born castes. The middle and low castes consist of Sudras and Harijans.
Calculated value of $\chi^2 = 10.78$, χ^2 at the .01 level of significance with 1 d.f. = 6.64.
a. Based on the third column in table 1.
b. Based on the share of each caste grouping in the non-Vaishya Hindu population of Vizag, as computed from the last column in table 1.

TABLE 4
Frequency Distribution of Non-Vaishya Hindu Entrepreneurs Born in Andhra Pradesh by Caste Ranking

Caste Ranking	Observed Frequency[a]	Expected Frequency[b]
Twice-born castes	14	7.3
Middle and low castes	14	20.7

NOTE: Calculated value of $\chi^2 = 8.32$, χ^2 at the .05 level of significance with 1 d.f. = 3.84.
a. Based on the first column in table 1.
b. Based on the share of each caste grouping in the non-Vaishya Hindu population of Vizag, as computed from the last column in table 1.

If the Hindu population in Vizag is divided into high castes (twice-born castes), middle castes (Sudras), and low castes (Harijans), there is a significant positive relationship between caste ranking, on the one hand, and education, income, occupational status, and perceived class and status, on the other.[4] Thus, as expected, the paternal economic status of entrepreneurs from twice-born castes was significantly higher than those of Sudras (table 5). Entrepreneurs were asked: "Was your father's economic status high, medium, or low?" Eleven high-caste entrepreneurs indicated a high paternal economic status, fifteen a medium status, and none a low status; two Sudras indicated a high status, eight a medium status, and four a low status (table 6).[5]

There were a number of differences between entrepreneurs from twice-born and middle castes that may result, in part, from the higher family economic status of the higher castes. The median initial equity capital of the firms of high-caste entrepreneurs was Rs. 60,000 (or about U.S.$8,000 at the official exchange rate), and fourteen of twenty-eight of them received the bulk of their initial capital from their families (ancestors, siblings, spouses, and descendants). In contrast, the median initial capital of the Sudras was only Rs. 37,500,[6] and only five of fifteen of them acquired initial funds from their families. The median and modal educational class for entrepreneurs from twice-born castes was a bachelor's degree, compared to a secondary certificate for Sudras. Only 20 percent of the Sudras have bachelor's degrees and 73 percent secondary certificates, compared to 57 and 89 percent respectively for the high-castes, entrepreneurs.[7] High caste families, with a disproportionate number of enterprises and con-

TABLE 5

Frequency Distribution of Hindu Entrepreneurs by Paternal Economic Status

Caste Ranking	Paternal Economic Status[a]	
	High	Middle or Low
Twice-born castes	11	15
Middle castes	2	12

NOTE: Calculated value of $\chi^2 = 9.39$, χ^2 at the .01 level of significance with 1 d.f. = 6.64.

a. Based on columns entitled "Economic Status of Father," table 6.

TABLE 6
Firms and Entrepreneurs

Caste/Birthplace	Number	Median Income Class[a]	Economic Status of Father			Major Occupation of Father[b]		Median Initial Capital	Median Education	Median Years Prior Management Experience[d]	Firms	
			High	Medium	Low	Business[c]	Nonbusiness				Median Value Added[e]	Median Employment Level[f]
Brahmin												
A.P.[g]	9	2,501-5,000	3	5	0	2	6	35,000	Bachelor's	6.0	62,300	12.0
Other	2	2,501-5,000	0	2	0	2	0	12,500	Bachelor's, master's	7.0	30,000	23.5
Total	11	2,501-5,000	3	7	0	4	6	30,000	Bachelor's	6.0	41,000	12.0
Kshatriya												
A.P.[g] (Total)	5	0-2,500	1	3	0	1	3	80,000	Secondary	16.0	37,500	15.0
Vaishya												
A.P.[g]	4	5,001-10,000	0	4	0	2	2	35,000	Secondary	3.0	37,500	11.0
Other	8	50,001 & above	7	1	0	8	0	425,000	Bachelor's	18.5	325,000	20.5
Total	12	50,001 & above	7	5	0	10	2	125,000	Some univ., bachelor's	13.0	105,000	12.0
Sudra												
A.P.[g]	14	5,001-10,000	2	7	4	7	7	30,000	Secondary	3.0	21,000	9.0
Other	1	10,001-25,000	0	1	0	0	1	70,000	Some secondary	0.0	230,000	16.0
Total	15	5,001-10,000	2	8	4	7	8	37,500	Secondary	2.0	28,000	10.0

Muslim											
A.P.[g]	4	2	0	2	1	5,001-10,000	21,000	Secondary	2.5	8,350	5.0
Other	3	1	0	1	2	5,001-10,000	20,000	Secondary	7.0	21,000	10.0
Total	7	3	0	3	3	5,001-10,000	20,000	Secondary	5.0	19,000	7.0
Other[h] Outside A.P.[g] (Total)	4	1	3	0	2	10,001-50,000	100,000	Bachelor's	10.0	94,000	40.0
Entire Sample											
A.P.[g]	36	21	4	14	19	5,001-10,000	35,000	Secondary, some univ.	5.5	37,500	12.0
Other	18	8	0	13	5	25,001-50,000	100,000	Bachelor's	10.0	122,500	18.0
Total	54	29	4	27	24	5,001-10,000	45,000	Some univ.	6.5	40,500	12.0
Total Twice-Born											
A.P.[g]	18	12	0	5	11	2,501-5,000	40,000	Secondary, some univ.	6.0	41,000	12.0
Other	10	3	0	10	0	50,001 & above	425,000	Bachelor's	13.0	160,000	20.5
Total	28	15	0	15	11	10,001-25,000	60,000	Bachelor's	9.0	50,000	13.0
Schumpeterian Entrepreneurs											
A.P.[g]	8	4	0	4	4	5,001-25,000	43,000	Some univ.	8.0	40,250	16.5
Other	9	2	0	6	3	50,001 & above	560,000	Bachelor's	23.0	450,000	56.0
Total	17	6	0	10	7	25,001-50,000	320,000	Bachelor's	13.0	62,500	21.0

a. Measured in rupees per annum (in fiscal year 1969/70).

b. The total number of responses may be less than the number of entrepreneurs because of cases where there is a lack of response or where the answer is unknown.

c. Business as a major occupation refers to the management and/or ownership of any business unless it is agricultural or professional.

d. Refers to the median experience in entrepreneurial and/or management positions (outside agriculture and the professions) prior to the establishment of the firm.

e. Refers to gross value added (in rupees), in the fiscal year 1969/70), which equals the value of output of a firm minus purchases from other firms.

f. Measured in terms of average number of full-time wage earners in the firm in fiscal year 1969/70.

g. Andhra Pradesh.

h. Includes Sikhs, Syrian Christians, Parsis.

nections with business friends, could more readily arrange management experience for their sons. Accordingly, the median prior management experience (defined in table 6, note d) of twice-born entrepreneurs was higher than for Sudras. Prior to the involvement in their present firms, the major previous occupation of twenty of the twenty-eight high-caste businessmen and only five of the fifteen Sudras involved entrepreneurial or managerial responsibility.[8] The lesser socioeconomic status, access to capital, educational achievement, entrepreneurial and management experience, and access to government of Sudra businessmen (as indicated in table 7) was associated with a lower level of entrepreneurial success and a smaller size firm than for businessmen from twice-born castes. The median gross value added of firms (value of output minus purchases from other firms) directed by high-caste entrepreneurs was Rs. 50,000 compared to Rs. 28,000 for Sudras. In addition, high-caste entrepreneurs were in a higher income bracket than middle-caste entrepreneurs. Although the differences diminish when comparisons are confined to those born within the state of Andhra Pradesh, high-caste businessmen still have more education, more management experience, more access to capital, a higher parental economic status, and larger firms, but not higher incomes (table 6).

Despite the lack of low-caste entrepreneurs, there were three Protestants, one Catholic, and one Harijan who were the top day-to-day managers of enterprises (usually on the technical rather than on the sales and personnel side). This is consistent with a pattern of a relatively high predisposition by members of low-caste communities in Vizag for salaried positions with a secure tenure and of a low propensity for self-employment. The risk of business activity is not attractive to Harijan castes, whose designation as "backward" castes entitles them to a portion of the quota of university seats and civil service positions (even though usually at the lower echelons). In addition, Harijans and Christians measure low in family income, access to capital, business experience, training, and education[9] (despite scheduled caste legislation in recent years). Furthermore, they lack connections in high government positions, a network of relationships within the business community, and (analogous to the black supervisor of white American workers) a secure psychocultural acceptance of their positions of authority.

Among the Sudra *jatis*, only the Kammas and Naidus, each with 2.27 percent of the population and 5.56 percent of the entrepreneurs

TABLE 7
Distribution of Government Assistance to Entrepreneurs

	Some Assistance	No Assistance
Caste		
Brahmin	7	4
Kshatriya	4	1
Vaishya	7	5
Sudra	6	9
Muslim	3	4
Other	2	2
TOTAL	29	25
Economic Status of the Father		
High	13	4
Medium	13	16
Low	1	3
Not available	2	2
TOTAL	29	25
Birthplace		
A.P.[a]	18	10
India outside A.P.[a]	9	13
Outside India	2	2
TOTAL	29	25
Educational Attainment[b]		
University	17	8
Secondary	9	11
Primary	3	6
TOTAL	29	25
Prior Experience		
Business background[c]	18	10
Nonbusiness background	9	13
None	2	2
TOTAL	29	25

NOTE: Government assistance included technical and management help, financial aid, and leasing or subsidized rental of land or building from government agencies (but not public firms).

a. Andhra Pradesh.

b. Indicates educational level completed.

c. "Business background" indicates that the major previous occupation of the entrepreneur prior to the establishment of the firm was in entrepreneurial and/or management position(s) (outside agriculture and the professions).

(i.e., three), were as highly represented in the sample as in the population as a whole. The Kammas, a sizeable and prosperous farming caste primarily in the coastal districts of Andhra, are together with the Reddis among the politically dominant castes in the state. Members of this caste have used their economic advantage, political access, and hard work to facilitate movement from farming and rural trade to business and the professions in the urban areas.[10] Interestingly enough, all three Kammas received financial assistance from government agencies, although only seven of the other entrepreneurs received this assistance. In addition, the median Kamma entrepreneur had more education, management experience, initial capital, and greater success than the median entrepreneur in the sample, despite the fact that all three had established their businesses after 1966. Because of the small number of sample Kammas, these findings can only be suggestive.

There was no separate Naidu *jati* before the twentieth century. Some of the Harijans and (as in the cases of the families of the three entrepreneurs) lower Sudras in Andhra who were upwardly mobile tried to escape discrimination by identifying as Naidu, considered a Sudra caste of some standing.[11]

Among twice-born castes, the Vaishya (mercantile) community, with about 22 percent of the entrepreneurs in comparison to about 2 percent of the population of Vizag, was especially well represented. Most of the Vaishyas were born out of state. In turn, eight of the eleven Hindu entrepreneurs born outside the state were from traditional business communities. The fathers of out-of-state Vaishyas have the highest economic status and the highest percentage (100 percent) engaged in management and/or ownership of nonagricultural business. This family background, in part, has enabled the Vaishyas from the outside to rank the highest in median education, median prior management experience, median initial capital, and in the percentage who have received the major share of their initial capital from other family members. Not surprisingly, if entrepreneurs were classified according to birthplace (whether in-state or out-of-state) and caste, out-of-state Vaishyas would have the highest median value added of the firm and highest median income (table 6).

Each of these eight Vaishya entrepreneurs, together with other members of their families, had at least five to ten business units scattered throughout India, while four of the families had more than twenty firms. Three entrepreneurs were Khatri, Sindhi (both men were refugees from West Pakistan in 1947), and Bhatia (a Gujarati trading caste initially from Kutch), major trading and financial communities with origins in the eighteenth century. Five in the sample were Marwaris, primarily from rural trading *jatis* in agriculture-poor Rajasthan. Although few Marwaris entered major urban manufacturing before World War I, several decades after the earliest indigenous industrial venture,[12] today they are the leading Indian business community. Under the umbrella of British military power during the colonial period, all four of these communities conducted entrepreneurial activity in alien linguistic or religious communities (the Khatri and Sindhi Hindus in Islamic northwestern undivided India, the Marwaris primarily in Calcutta, and the Bhatias in Bombay).[13]

Outsiders from specialized business communities were not expected to participate in the network of traditional obligations or to become local community members. Prior to independence, these communities, including the eight business families, entered sectors of trade and finance (and in a few cases after World War I even manufacturing) that, by and large, did not compete with British industrial interests. Several of the large industrial families in the sample used their control of banks to fund their own enterprises. The families in banking and commerce amassed capital and business experience. They used these to make substantial moves into manufacturing (in some cases buying existing enterprises from the British) after independence in 1947, when conditions—increased protection of industry, the accompanying decline of trade, and the more favorable government policy toward indigenous enterprise—were propitious for doing so. For example, A. R. Balchandani (a pseudonym), a radio importer in the 1940s and 1950s, switched to the manufacture of electronic components and other radio parts in Madras and Vizag in the 1960s after increased forms of protection restricted the supply of imported radios. Although the Indian political elite was less favorably inclined toward private capitalism than the British and less accessible to outsiders, at the state level the economic power of the major business communities and families was sufficiently well established and the economic resources sufficiently abundant that the entrepreneurs could pull the political levers essential to insure the security and expansion of their business interests.

Gradually they moved beyond major industrial cities such as Calcutta and Bombay to establish manufacturing firms in many of the other cities in India, including Visakhapatnam in the 1960s. These leading families continued control of the far-flung industrial empire despite the abolition of the managing agency system (where two or more legally separate companies are controlled by a single managing firm) in 1970 and the legislation designed to restrict the expansion of large business houses. The country-wide network of firms maintained a "community of interest" through the ties between family members who held management and ownership interest in the various enterprises. In fact, the companies frequently were controlled by one or two principals in the family who for tax purposes dispersed the ownership of enterprises in the names of other family members. Large business families, because of their accumulation of resources, knowledge, organizational skill, and influence, were most likely to receive licenses for the establishment of a new enterprise or the acquisition of materials, and were in a better position to take advantage of government schemes to encourage small industry and geographical diversification. Frequently large industrial houses owned a series of "small-scale" industrial enterprises, which under other institutional arrangements would be described as branches of a large-scale enterprise based in a large manufacturing city. In two instances in the sample a large industrial house prevented from establishing new enterprises without an explicit industrial license was able to purchase an establishment that had already been granted a license.

Generally, the leading member of a major business family remained in Calcutta, Bombay, or Delhi, except for occasional visits to firms elsewhere. Other members of the family were posted in other cities to oversee the construction of the plant and establishment of the enterprise. When production became routine, the day-to-day management of the firm was left to professional managers. Family members would make periodic visits, especially when crises arose or decisions about expansion needed to be made.

The large business family, because of its wealth and financial security, has the latitude to provide for the training, education, travel, and business experience of its sons, and can afford the purchase of the plant and equipment that is most appropriate for the young businessman's entrepreneurial development. As youngsters, the sons learn the nature of the enterprises and are exposed to a business milieu. They are generally enrolled in prestigious schools, frequently encouraged to study law, economics, engineering, or business administration at the university, and afforded foreign travel and training where advantageous. A family with several sons may try to diversify their main academic fields among subjects relevant for business, so that the backgrounds are complementary. During school vacations and after graduation each son is moved from job to job within the family's firms, gradually having his responsibility increased so that in his early twenties he may be in charge of the day-to-day operations at one of the plants, and a few years later he may be entrusted to make major decisions in a plant in a minor industrial city (such as Vizag) away from the family's headquarters. Marriage may be arranged in part to further an economic alliance with another large business family.

Manufacturing units in Visakhapatnam had only a peripheral role in determining the overall business success of these families. Despite the fact that seven of the eight entrepreneurs had a 1969/70 annual personal income exceeding Rs. 50,000, four of the eight entrepreneurs were incurring business losses from their manufacturing units in Vizag. Although the size of the firms was substantial when compared to others in the sample, the firms were small when compared to other enterprises of the entrepreneur in other parts of India. Among the firms where information was available and which had existed for over five years, the rates of growth in employment and production for out-of-state Vaishya firms were substantially less than for the rest of the sample. Three out of four of these firms declined in output and employment in the five years previous to 1969/70, while one had an increase in both categories. In contrast, among other firms, fourteen grew in output, two remained the same, and three declined; in employment, eleven increased, six stayed constant, and two declined.

In India, the licensing of capacity and materials to specific firms is done by the state government. The evidence concerning growth, profits, and capacity utilization is consistent with the contention that most large business houses acquired licenses to establish factories in Vizag (one of the cities in less-industrialized states favored by government policy) not so much for purposes of expansion, but to obtain licensed imports and materials, undertake transfers of these to sister firms, and protect a market position by foreclosing the growth of licensed capacity by other competitors in the industry.[14]

Sikh entrepreneurs, from Khatri trading communities originating in northwestern undivided India, shared many of the characteristics of Hindu Khatri businessmen and other out-of-state Vaishyas, including a disproportionate representation among sample entrepreneurs and a high degree of business success. Both Sikhs were expatriates from neighboring countries, and exhibited the qualities of thoroughness, diligence, drive, capacity for adjustment, and receptivity to new ideas that Nair observed among the uprooted Sikhs.[15]

From early in the Christian era, local trading communities have been active in Andhra, especially near the political centers and temple towns. There is some evidence that the merchant castes attained their high ritual and social status as a result of the vital service they rendered to the ruling dynasties and the priestly class. Komatis (the local name for Vaishyas) comprise over one-half of the traders in Vizag city.[16] However, unlike Vaishyas in many other parts of India, Komatis have virtually no experience in manufacturing. Coastal Andhra, because of its comparative advantage in agriculture, its deficiency in power resources and basic raw materials, its lack of a number of social overhead services, and the relative neglect of its economic development when part of Madras state until 1953, has long been backward industrially, and thus has never developed an indigenous industrial community. Although Vaishyas are disproportionately represented among in-state entrepreneurs, their income class and firm value added were not even above the median of entrepreneurs born in Andhra.[17] Their low ranking in business success may be related to their relatively low family economic status, which is associated with low educational attainment, business experience, and initial capital resources (table 6). Two of the four entrepreneurs had fathers involved in business, but the business of only one, a manufacturer of iron hardware whose father had traded the commodity, was related to that of his father or was assisted by him.

For the Brahmins, merchant and industrial entrepreneurship is far removed from the traditional caste occupations of priesthood, teaching, the professions, and government service. Relatively few of the fathers of Brahmin entrepreneurs were involved in business and none were engaged in the same business as the son (table 6). Yet it is not surprising that the major previous occupation of five of eleven was trade and sales, or that 50 percent of the businessmen with an entrepreneurial background in commerce were Brahmins. For prospective industrialists with a lack of personal or familial expertness and capital, investment and experience in petty trade is a natural stepping stone to a larger, more fixed, and more complex manufacturing enterprise.

Nor is it surprising that a disproportionate number of these entrepreneurs acquired their initial capital from their own resources (i.e., seven of eleven compared to only twenty of forty-three from the rest of the sample) and that their median initial capital was below the sample median. Since none could obtain their start in a relative's business, they obtained prior experience and (in some cases) capital as merchants (four), engineers or technicians (three), or sales managers (one) in the same industries they established, or as professionals (two). Nevertheless, the median value added of their firms is as large as that of the sample. Perhaps this is partially associated with their high level of education, as 72.7 percent of them have at least a bachelor's degree, compared to only 46.3 percent of the sample as a whole. Their median income is below the median. This may be related to the fact that as many as seven Brahmins were involved in only one business.

The fact that Brahmin participation in industrial entrepreneurial activity in Vizag is about as high as their percentage in the population may result from several "push" and "pull" factors. Major "push" factors have been the administrative orders after World War I which limited the number of Brahmins in government departments, and the scheduled caste legislation after independence which discriminated against high castes. The increase in the status of industrial entrepreneurship accompanying the inducements to indigenous small-scale industry in the independence period and the wealth and influence available to facilitate investment in training and new enterprises are "pull" factors. Apparently, however, Brahmins are not as relatively well represented in industrial entrepreneurial activity as in Tamil Nadu, where the "push" factor is greater as a result of more vigorous anti-Brahmin measures in the government sector, and where the "pull" factor is more powerful, because of the substantial wealth accumulated by Brahmins, especially in land, in the colonial period.[18]

Table 1 indicates that Brahmins are substantially underrepresented among blue-collar workers in Vizag. Owens,[19] in his study of industrialists in Howrah, West Bengal, even suggests that entrepreneurs from the Brahmin and other upper castes are unwilling to do onerous manual labor. I found no evidence that Brahmins who are entrepreneurs in Vizag are any less inclined than other entrepreneurs to do dirty manual work when that is required in their unit. Brahmins, with a high ritual status, long tradition of literacy, and a background of relative privilege, do have an aversion to low-status, demeaning, and ritually polluting work, but not to physical labor in relatively high-status activity, such as industrial entrepreneurship.

The proportionate representation of Muslims in entrepreneurial activity in Vizag is almost as high as for the Vaishyas. Perhaps Muslim participation can be explained partly because of limited alternatives in the civil service, and the absence of traditional barriers to occupations that are polluting to Hindus, such as shoemaking and rope manufacturing. For M. C. Ahmad, who was an administrative head in a coastal Andhran district in old Madras state, and whose father was police superintendent in the former Muslim-led princely state of Mysore, past wealth and influence stemmed a decline in options in government service in the 1950s and 1960s by facilitating two industrial ventures in Vizag. However, none of the other six Muslim entrepreneurs, four of whom were born within the state, had ties with the old Muslim ruling class of the princely states. Local Muslim entrepreneurs, like local Muslims in general, did not enjoy a high parental economic status or high educational status. In Vizag, the caste status of Muslims was relatively low, although not well defined nor as low as for Harijans and Christians.[20] This socioeconomic background may have been partially responsible for the low level of initial capital, value added, and income associated with Muslim business endeavors.

BIRTHPLACE

The birthplaces of entrepreneurs were divided equally between Vizag District, the state of Andhra Pradesh outside Vizag District, and South Asia outside Andhra Pradesh. The percentage born outside the state was over five times their share of the population of Vizag City by place of birth (table 8),[21] and others born outside Vizag District were also disproportionately represented (table 9). This is not surprising, since there is less regional segmentation in the market for high-level manpower, such as entrepreneurs, than for ordinary labor.

Those born outside of Andhra Pradesh were most successful and those born within Vizag District generally least successful as entrepreneurs (table 9). The four entrepreneurs born outside India's present borders—three who were refugees from West Pakistan in 1947 and one who left Burma as a result of business nationalization in 1965—were among thirteen entrepreneurs in the top two income classes and their firms were all among the top ten in value added.

Why were entrepreneurs from outside the state more successful than

TABLE 8
Frequency Distribution of Entrepreneurs by Birthplace

Birthplace	Observed Frequency[a]	Expected Frequency[b]
Andhra Pradesh	36	50.8
Outside Andhra Pradesh	18	3.2

NOTE: Calculated value of χ^2 = 72.76, χ^2 at the .01 level of significance with 1 d.f. = 6.64.
a. Based on table 9, column 2.
b. Based on table 9, column 1.

TABLE 9
Sample Entrepreneurs and Population of Vizag

Birthplace	Birthplace of Population of Vizag City (%)	Birthplace of Sample Entrepreneurs (%)	Median Value Added of Firms by Birthplace of Sample Entrepreneur[a]	Median Income Class of Entrepreneurs by Birthplace[a]
Vizag City	58.2	24.1	37,000	2,501–10,000
Vizag District outside city	20.8	9.3	22,500	2,501–10,000
A.P.[b] outside Vizag District	15.1	33.3	61,500	0–5,000
India outside A.P.[b]	5.9	25.9	42,000	10,001–50,000
Pakistan[c]	—[d]	5.4	450,000	25,001–50,000
Burma	—[d]	1.9	1,688,000	25,001–50,000
TOTAL	100.0	99.9[e]		

a. Measured in rupees per annum (in fiscal year 1969/70).
b. Andhra Pradesh
c. Postpartition borders are used to allocate individuals born in undivided India.
d. Less than .05 percent.
e. May not add up to 100 percent because of rounding.

entrepreneurs from within the state? Due to financial, psychological, and linguistic barriers to interstate migration, entrepreneurs were not likely to immigrate without some wealth and education, and the prospect for substantial economic advantage. Thus, outside entrepreneurs who migrated to Vizag, a city which lacked local industrial skills and experience, originated from a select portion of the population, as the sample totals on caste, class, education, initial capital, and business experience show (table 6). In addition, the challenge of a new environment to immigrants may have had a beneficial educational and psychological effect in breaking tradition and enhancing innovation and success. A related factor was that the geographical dispersion of friends, relatives, and neighbors of the migrants may have allowed the rejection of local values, obligations, and sanctions, such as notions of caste propriety, which impeded rational business practice.[22]

In Vizag, the percentage of industrial entrepreneurs from outside the state is 33⅓ percent compared to 29 percent of the trading entrepreneurs in Rao's sample, despite the fact that industrial activity involves a longer gestation period of investment and a greater extent of fixed capital than trade. Perhaps the percentage of immigrant industrialists relative to traders results from the fact that individuals in high-income brackets are more likely to have access to the resources to migrate and comprise a higher percentage of industrialists than traders, and because of the fact that greater economies of agglomeration in manufacturing mean that opportunities in industry are more centralized in urban centers such as Vizag.

PATERNAL ECONOMIC STATUS

The 1969/70 median income of the entrepreneur divided by the median number of dependents, five, was Rs. 1,000–2,000, substantially above Rs. 589.3, the 1969/70 all-India average income per capita[23] (which exceeds the all-India median income). Responses by entrepreneurs indicated that the economic status of the fathers was high in the aggregate (table 6). This is despite the fact that respondents judged the status of unskilled factory workers as low, even though it is at least medium when one considers that 70 percent of India's working population is in the low-income agricultural sector. Table 10 reinforces this view of the economic status of fathers, since 20 percent were in cultivation, 2 percent in agricultural labor, and 78 percent in nonagricultural pursuits compared to 50 percent, 20 percent, and 30 percent

TABLE 10

Distribution of Fathers of Entrepreneurs in Economic Sector

Sector	Major Activities of Fathers of Entrepreneurs (%)	Working Population of India, 1951 (%)
Cultivation	20	50
Agricultural labor	2	20
Mining, manufacturing, household industries, etc.	29	12
Construction	14	1
Trade and commerce	14	5
Transport and communications	0	2
Other services	22	10
TOTAL	101[a]	99[a]

SOURCES: The author's sample, and Tata Economic Consultancy Services, *Statistical Outline of India 1970* (Bombay: Popular Prakashan, 1970), p. 16.

a. Column may not add up to 100 percent because of rounding.

respectively in India's working population in 1951.[24] In addition, the major occupation of twenty-seven of fifty-one of the fathers was some form of nonagricultural business (table 6).

The economic status of the father was closely related to the entrepreneurial success of the son (table 11). As discussed below, a high paternal economic status assists the prospective entrepreneurs in acquiring resources for investment in education (table 12), training, and plant and equipment, and in obtaining business experience and government assistance.

THE STATUS OF SCHUMPETERIAN ENTREPRENEURS

It can be suggested that the high caste and paternal economic status of the entrepreneur results from the fact that the entrepreneur is designated as one who commits ownership capital. If the entrepreneur need not necessarily be a capitalist, one might argue that he might be more likely to arise from a lower socioeconomic background. Schumpeter, for example, contends that entrepreneurs arise from all economic classes.[25] Might the Schumpeterian entrepreneur, the innovator, be more likely to originate from a lower class and caste than the entrepreneur chosen according to Knight's definition?

TABLE 11
1969/70 Income Class of Entrepreneurs

Income Class of Entrepreneur[a]	Economic Status of Father			
	Low	Medium	High	NA[b]
2,500 or less	3	6	0	1
2,501–10,000	1	11	2	1
10,001–50,000	0	10	6	0
50,001 or more	0	1	7	0
Not available	0	1	2	2
TOTAL	4	29	17	4

NOTE: Where Y is net income class (1 for less than 0, 2 for 0–2,500, 3 for 2,501–5,000, 4 for 5,001–10,000, 5 for 10,001–25,000, 6 for 25,001–50,000, and 7 for 50,001 or more), X_1 is father's economic status (1 for low, 2 for medium, and 3 for high) and X_2 is the entrepreneur's age (in years), $Y = 1.1353 + 1.389X_1 + 0.0071X_2$, $t_1 = 2.3082$, and the multiple regression coefficient on X_1 is significant at the 5 percent level.
a. Measured in rupees per annum (in fiscal year 1969/70).
b. Not available.

TABLE 12
Educational Achievement of Entrepreneurs

Education Completed by Entrepreneur	Economic Status of Father			
	Low	Medium	High	NA[a]
Primary	2	4	1	2
Secondary	1	13	6	0
University	1	12	10	2
TOTAL	4	29	17	4

NOTE: There is a positive correlation between the economic status of the fathers and the education of the entrepreneurs. Where Y is educational achievement (0 for none, 1 for some primary, 2 for primary, 3 for some secondary, 4 for secondary, 5 for some university, 6 for a bachelor's degree, 7 for a master's degree, 8 for above a master's degree) and X is the economic status of the father (see table 11), $Y = 3.13083 + 0.72100X$, $t = 2.15510$, and the regression coefficient is significant at the 5 percent level.
a. Not available.

The socioeconomic background of persons from sample firms who carried out "new combinations" in the coastal Andhran economy (see Appendix B) was even higher than that of the fifty-four sample entrepreneurs. Innovators had a higher paternal economic status than that of entrepreneurs as a whole, as ten of sixteen innovators indicated their status as high and none indicated it was low (table 6). The over-representation of twice-born Hindu castes (59 percent of the innovators), Muslims (18 percent), and Sikhs (12 percent) was more, and the underrepresentation of other Hindu castes (i.e., one Sudra) was less, among the seventeen Schumpeterian entrepreneurs than among the sample as a whole. Two innovators were Khatri Sikhs, one was a Marwari, one a Bhatia, one a Sindhi, and one a Parsi (all important Indian business communities). The median levels of management experience, education, and initial capital of the entrepreneur,[26] and the percentage of the fathers of the entrepreneurs in business among Schumpeterian entrepreneurs, are higher than for sample entrepreneurs as a whole, whether the figures refer to in-state, out-of-state, or all entrepreneurs. Finally, five of the innovators were from firms which were in the top ten firms of the sample according to value added, and six innovators were among thirteen entrepreneurs in the top two income classes. Schumpeterian entrepreneurs ranked higher than the sample as a whole in median income, and in median value added and employment of the firms, regardless of whether the comparisons were made for entrepreneurs from Andhra Pradesh, from other states, or in total (table 6).[27]

There may be reason to expect the Schumpeterian entrepreneur to originate from a class and caste background as high as entrepreneurs in the Knight framework. One must recall that an idea, technique, or invention needs to be put into business practice before it becomes an innovation. The opportunities to arrive at new business ideas are not distributed randomly within a population, but are partly dependent upon the availability of training, education, information, facilities, access to creative associates, and other advantages, all expedited by wealth and position.[28] The carrying out of ideas and inventions also depends upon access to funds and influence. Their availability to the innovator is especially vital in a country like India, with a poorly developed capital market, and a low propensity to provide capital for projects initiated outside the family, cian, or *jati*.

The findings and explanations concerning the higher socioeconomic status of Schumpeterian entrepreneurs in this sample can, however, only be suggestive. First, the sample of innovators is small. In the second place, all the Schumpeterian entrepreneurs (and their families) had to take the responsibility for providing the initial capital for the firm which embodied the innovation (see Appendix B). In large firms, such as joint stock companies, where innovation is more institutionalized, or in economies more advanced than India where legal, social, and economic sanctions, and networks of relationships foster a wider market for loans and investment, innovation may not be as dependent upon the availability of capital from the entrepreneur's family. More research is needed before we can have a clear view of the socioeconomic origins of Schumpeterian entrepreneurs in various types of enterprises, sectors, and economies.

CONCLUSION

Evidence from other studies in South Asia supports my findings on the caste and class origins of entrepreneurs. However, because most of the authors to be cited do not ask questions concerning the differential socioeconomic background of the entrepreneur and the general population, they often fail to point out the high class and caste status of businessmen.

In the selection of evidence from other works, I am focusing on the difference between the socioeconomic status of businessmen and the population as a whole, since there is widespread agreement, even among those who contend that entrepreneurs are upwardly mobile, that *among sample entrepreneurs* there is a positive relationship between the socioeconomic statuses of respondents and their fathers.[29] I am not aware of other studies which compare the percentage distribution of entrepreneurs and the general population in India by caste and paternal economic status. There are, however, a number of studies of Indian industrialists which point to a concentration of entrepreneurial activity among the sons of the members of the large business houses, who represent a small fraction of the population.[30] Although Berna remarks on the extremely varied backgrounds of sample industrialists in the state of Tamil Nadu, forty-one of the forty-six Hindu entrepreneurs with some caste designation (excluding the three designated by social community, not always indicative of caste) are from twice-born castes, and the rest are Sudras.[31] A highly disproportionate number of the fathers of manufacturing entrepreneurs in Pakistan, which had a common history with India before 1947, were from traditional business communities while a low percentage of fathers were in wage employment or agriculture. Contrary to Papanek's interpretation, this pattern would suggest that the socioeconomic class status of entrepreneurs was high when compared to the population.[32] Indigenous managers of large public, foreign, and private enterprises in India also originate from a highly select portion of the population, since none of the fathers were laborers, only 10 percent were farmers (all of whom were small farm operators or large farm owners), and the rest were white-collar workers, government officials, business executives, professional men, and business owners.[33] Adding a perspective to the social origin of businessmen is a study of factory laborers in Poona indicating no significant difference between the caste and social community of the workers and the city population.[34]

The weight of the evidence suggests that industrial business activity in India, rather than being a path for substantial upward socioeconomic mobility, is a way of maintaining or defending privileged status, and enhancing or consolidating the high economic position of the family. In the final chapter, I suggest that the high socioeconomic status of entrepreneurs may be found not only in India but probably also in most of the rest of the nonsocialist world.

See Appendix B for additional information for chapter 4.

5

EDUCATION, TRAINING, OCCUPATIONAL BACKGROUND, AND INITIAL CAPITAL

THIS chapter investigates the nature of the relationship between education, training, occupational background, and sources and amounts of initial capital, on the one hand, and the entry, success, and behavior of entrepreneurs, on the other. Education, training, and experience can increase the supply and success of entrepreneurs by making available more skills which are suitable for manufacturing or can decrease the supply by increasing the options of persons in alternative endeavors. Superior access to capital for starting new enterprises increases the supply and success of entrepreneurs.

In addition, despite a somewhat different emphasis from the previous chapter, this chapter presents further evidence concerning the effect of a privileged family background on the supply and success of entrepreneurs.

OCCUPATIONAL BACKGROUND

By virtue of being engaged in the manufacturing sector, entrepreneurs rarely pursued the traditional caste-assigned occupations. The superior efficiency and market power of modern capitalistic firms undercut the viability of caste-assigned craft enterprises, and impelled most self-employed persons to seek another occupation in the capitalist sector. In the sample, only seven Vaishyas who had previously been involved in trade and a Kshatriya previously in agriculture participated in the traditional caste vocation. The movement away from this started one generation before, as only eleven of the fathers were involved in the caste occupation.

However, in almost one-half of the cases (twenty-six of fifty-four) there was a close link between an occupation of the entrepreneurs and their fathers—nine in the same line of manufacturing, three in the same type of trade, three in a similar kind of construction business, one in the mining business, one in government service, two in mechanics, three in manufacturing a product sold in their fathers' trading enterprises, two in manufacturing a good pursued as a sideline in their fathers' construction firms, one in a port enterprise, and one where the son became secretary of a jute merchants' association, of which his father was a member.

Much of the focus in the remainder of the section is on the extent to which the prior economic activity of the entrepreneur prepared him in undertaking his present industrial activity. Thirty-two of fifty-four entrepreneurs have had some previous work experience in the same industry (i.e., where at least one of the products was the same as one of the products of his present firm)—eight as manufacturing entrepreneurs, eight as commercial entrepreneurs or managers, four as contractors, and twelve as manufacturing employees. This does not include four entrepreneurs whose family members or wife's family had experience with one of the products being produced, and two entrepreneurs with business experience in manufacturing though not in the same industry. For many entrepreneurs (and their families), the manufacturing business entailed a step-by-step progression, and not a sharp break, from less complex economic activities with which they were familiar.

Table 13 indicates the disproportionate prior involvement of entrepreneurs in nonagricultural sectors—96.0 percent of entrepreneurs compared to 30.5 percent of the working population of India. If entrepreneurs are classified according to the sector of their major prior economic activity, the largest number, fourteen of fifty, was engaged in each of two sectors, manufacturing and the "other services" sector. In manufacturing, the main previous activity of seven of the entrepreneurs was management, of which five were involved in firms in which they were at least part owners. The family background of the seven expedited their movement into major entrepreneurial positions in manufacturing early in their career. Former manufacturers ranked first (among four major occupational groups) in paternal economic status (four of seven fathers were of high status), in the percentage of pater-

TABLE 13
Distribution of Economic Activities

Sector	Major Previous Activities of Entrepreneurs[a] (%)	Working Population (%) Vizag District 1961	Working Population (%) India 1961	Major Activities of Fathers of Entrepreneurs[b] (%)	Working Population (%) India 1931
Cultivation	4.0	71.6[c]	52.8	19.6	45.1
Agricultural labor	0.0	—	16.7	2.0	24.8
Mining, fishing, etc.	2.0	2.5	2.7	2.0	5.2
Household industries	2.0	6.5	6.4	3.9	—[d]
Manufacturing industries	28.0	2.5	4.2	23.5	8.9
Construction	14.0	0.6	1.1	13.7	1.0
Trade and commerce	22.0	3.9	4.1	13.7	5.6
Transport and communications	0.0	1.8	1.6	0.0	1.0
Other services	28.0	10.4	10.4	21.6	8.4
TOTAL	100.0	99.8[e]	100.0	100.0	100.0

SOURCES: Government of India, Census 1961—Andhra Pradesh, District Census Handbook: Visakhapatnam District, p. A27, and K. K. Dewett; G. C. Singh; and J. D. Varna, Indian Economics (Delhi: S. Chand & Co., 1970), p. 45, for data on the working population.
a. Four of the fifty-four entrepreneurs had no occupation prior to entering their present firms.
b. No information is available for three of the fathers.
c. Those in agricultural labor are included in cultivation.
d. Household industries are included in manufacturing industries.
e. Columns may not add up to 100 percent because of rounding.

nal involvement in business (six of seven), in the proportion receiving at least some of their initial capital from other family members (five), in median initial capital (Rs. 100,000), and in median management experience (seventeen years). The median educational level, some university education, was the same as that for the sample but below those formerly in commerce and in contracting. Since most of these entrepreneurs were well established, with wide managerial experience in manufacturing, sizeable capital resources, and substantial financial and technical assistance from other family members, it is not surprising that former manufacturers had the highest median income class and median value added of the firm, (Rs. 125,000 compared to a sample median of Rs. 40,500) (table 14).

Among entrepreneurs whose major previous occupation involved entrepreneurial or managerial responsibility, the largest number, ten, had been engaged in trade and sales. In the sample, entrepreneurs with a trading background are second to those with a manufacturing background in median income class and third in the median value added of the firm (table 14).[1] Those with commercial origins came from families with a high paternal economic status (a close second to former manufacturers) and a great deal of business experience (the major occupation of five of the nine fathers was business) but with little experience in manufacturing (the major activity of only one of the fathers). In addition, former traders had the highest median educational attainment and a high median number of years of prior management and/or entrepreneurial experience, 13 years (compared to a median of 6.5 years). The background in trade gave the entrepreneur a familiarity with the market, some general management and commercial experience, sales outlets and contacts, and some capital. Perhaps because of the availability of liquid capital from previous trading endeavors, the percentage of initial capital from family members was low. (Four of the ten received at least some capital from their family, the lowest proportion in this comparison of entrepreneurs in different occupational activities.) Median initial capital, Rs. 37,500 (third among occupational groups), was low. The fact that former traders tended to be involved in light manufacturing with some continuity with their previous occupation (becoming industrialists in a step-by-step process) may help to account for the low median initial capital.

Many of the former traders entered manufacturing to insure a regular source of supply or as a result of the perception of increased op-

TABLE 14
Major Previous Occupations of the Entrepreneurs

Previous Occupation	Total Number	Entrepreneurs				Median Income Class[a]	Median Value Added of Firms[a]
		From Twice-born Hindu Castes	Sudra	Muslim	Other		
Employment[b] (in the same industry)	12	3	6	3	0	5,001–10,000	18,250
Employment[b] (in a different industry)	1	0	1	0	0	0–2,500	3,000
Trade and sales	10	8	1	0	1	10,000–25,000	73,000
Manufacturing	7	7	0	0	0	25,001–50,000	125,000
Contracting	6	2	2	0	2	5,001–10,000	93,500
Professional	3	1	1	1	0	10,001–25,000	180,000
Government service	3	0	1	2	0	0–2,500	12,000
Agriculture	2	2	0	0	0	0–2,500	32,500
Applied arts	2	1	1	0	0	NA[c]	NA[c]
Other (banking, clerical, mining & services)	4	2	1	1	0	25,001–50,000	140,000
None	4	2	1	0	1	5,001–25,000	22,500
Entire sample	54	28	15	7	4	5,001–10,000	40,500

a. Measured in rupees per annum (in fiscal year 1969/70).
b. Refers to a job with little or no entrepreneurial or managerial responsibility.
c. Not available.

portunities for profits in industry relative to trade. The major catalyst for this shift was deliberate post-Independence government policy to encourage import substitution in manufacturing through higher tariffs, tighter import quotas, and industrial policy to encourage the use of domestic inputs. Three non-Andhra Vaishya families, who had been previously engaged in commerce that supported the interests of the British colonial government and foreign industrial capitalists, moved into large-scale manufacturing in the 1950s and 1960s after the Indian government had taken measures to encourage indigenous industry and discourage import trade.

Beginning in 1938, C. V. Shah worked as an agent and later as a franchise operator in a European-owned distribution station in Bombay for liquid-petroleum gas, gas cylinders, and gas stoves that had been imported from Europe. Between 1942 and 1957, Mr. Shah and his partners gradually bought the foreign enterprises for importing the cylinders and stoves and distributing the domestically produced liquid-petroleum gas in a number of major cities in western India. In the late 1950s, the 1960s, and the early 1970s, partly as a result of well-established business relations with large foreign petroleum firms, the economic interests of the Shah group grew vertically with the establishment of enterprises to manufacture and assemble gas stoves and ranges and their parts in western India, and horizontally with the setting up of distributorships and manufacturing firms in gas, cylinders, stoves, and related products in southern and eastern cities such as Vizag. Another example of an entrepreneur who moved from trade to manufacturing in the independence era was A. R. Balchandani, discussed in the previous chapter.

The seven former traders who were not out-of-state Vaishyas established much smaller manufacturing enterprises and are responsible for the fact that median initial capital and measures of entrepreneurial success are lower than for former manufacturers. Perhaps the chief illustration of a shift from import trade to industry among the seven is P. C. Govinda, an importer and seller of corks and aeromatic chemicals in Madras from 1930 to 1965, who founded a unit to produce corks in 1965 in response to the stricter quotas on imported corks. A few of the seven encountered difficulties in setting up a production line, coordinating the activities of a sizeable labor force, and cultivating the political ties sometimes essential for obtaining controlled inputs.

The literature on entrepreneurship discusses a "trader mentality" which results in an "irrational" preference for the quick turnover in commerce to the long-run returns in manufacturing.[2] Yet it would hardly seem irrational, given the management and technical skill of the entrepreneur and the nature of the business milieu, social overhead services, and government policies, for an entrepreneur to prefer trade to manufacturing as a result of a higher expected rate of return to his investment and time. This analysis of sample industrialists who originated in trade is useful in indicating some changes that tip the scales from trade to manufacturing. For some, an industrial venture awaited business experience and the accumulation of capital. Commercial entrepreneurship was perhaps the most suitable endeavor for acquiring these. For most, the decision to shift to manufacturing followed after deliberate changes in government policy enhanced the relative attractiveness of industry.

The six entrepreneurs whose major prior activity was contracting are second in the median value added of the firm, and tied for third in median income class. Contracting experience enabled the prospective industrialist to acquire capital, business experience and techniques, and a unique perspective on purchases of inputs and sales of outputs. After a few years of developing contracting, construction and fabrication skills, several of the respondents, who were dissatisfied with the work of subcontractors and the acute shortage of certain products gained insight into industrial opportunities and started manufacturing enterprises.

The major prior occupation of thirteen of the entrepreneurs was some form of employment, as opposed to an occupation involving entrepreneurial or management experience. Former employees ranked lowest among the four occupational groups in the percentage of fathers whose major activity was business, in the percentage receiving most of their initial capital from other family members, in median prior entrepreneurial and management experience, in median educational attainment, in median initial capital (Rs. 21,000 compared to a sample median of Rs. 45,000), and near the lowest in paternal economic status. However, seven of the thirteen received some initial capital from other family members, a proportion second among major occupational groups, but a virtual necessity for many in light of their relatively low earnings from previous work and their lack of credit standing.

A relatively large percentage of former employees became entrepreneurs because of "push" factors such as the lack of attractive options or the threat of persistent unemployment, rather than "pull" factors, such as the prospects of rapidly expanding markets. Seven of the employees, at the time of their severance, were with very small firms having a net worth of less than Rs. 8,000, compared to a (January 1971) median of Rs. 110,000 for sample firms. Because of their lack of economic viability, wages and employment security in very small firms are low. In fact, two of the former employees faced unemployment for longer than three months prior to establishing the sample firms, one because of an injury and another because of the collapse of the firm. Through scraping together small sums of initial capital (a median of Rs. 11,000 for former workers in these very small firms) from friends, relatives, and past earnings, the entrepreneur believed he could establish a cottage enterprise where his labor and management earnings would exceed his wages as a hired laborer. Even when returns to capital are included, the median income class of these seven entrepreneurs was Rs. 2,501–5,000 per annum, probably not much above the median income for India.[3]

Despite their and their families' lack of business experience, entrepreneurs with a professional background, with the advantage of access to capital from a well-to-do family and/or from professional earnings, and with the highest median initial capital and educational achievement of all occupational groups, were highly successful (table 14). The two former professionals with the greatest success had previously been partners in law firms which handled cases for business clients in Andhra Pradesh. This experience gave both a unique perspective on business opportunities in Andhra Pradesh and skill and knowledge concerning applications for quotas on inputs.

The largest sector, agriculture, with 72 percent of the population of Vizag District, contributed only 4 percent of entrepreneurs, who ranked low in terms of success (tables 13 and 14). Except for landowners, very few in the farm sector have the surplus available to invest in industry. But the low representation of landlords can be attributed to the high value they place on consumption and real estate expenditure, and their lack of experience in managing and coordinating a production process with specialized work tasks and machinery, and in secondary labor relations.

Entrepreneurs with a background in government service had little representation (5.6 percent) and ranked close to the bottom in terms of success (table 14). Other studies on Indian entrepreneurship would indicate a relatively small percentage of entrepreneurs with government background compared to other mixed less-developed economies such as Nigeria.[4] Most potentially capable entrepreneurs in the civil service have relatively high salaries, good working conditions, attractive fringe benefits, and secure tenure. The cost of severing a government job to enter entrepreneurial activity, which involves substantial risk, can be high. Also of importance is the type of link between the government and business sectors. In India, the bourgeoisie appears to be weaker relative to the bureaucracy and political elite than in other mixed economies such as the United States and Nigeria. In the United States, corporate officials cement ties and influence policies with government, in part, by moving to and from strategic positions in the Departments of Defense, Treasury, Commerce, and Agriculture. In Nigeria, political position and government service have enhanced the business prospects of individuals under both the civilian and military regimes.[5] In India, links between government and business are less direct, and the use of influence and position in one sector to enhance one's prospects in the other sector less frequent. In comparison to the United States and Nigeria, few private businessmen in India are a part of the ruling elite. Indeed, most businessmen, especially in the small-scale sector, exist at the sufferance of the political-bureaucratic leadership. In some instances, the price for obtaining political access and business security may be concessions, favors, and political loyalty.

Entrepreneurs with no prior work experience did surprisingly well, with a median income class above the sample median. Three of the four entrepreneurs started businesses in which their family or spouse's family had previous experience.

For convenience of discussion, I define a Type II entrepreneur as an entrepreneur in only one firm where the major output was manufactured goods, and where the firm employs less than ten workers *and* has assets of less than Rs. 40,000 annually, for three consecutive years. The corresponding Type II firm tends to be a unit with simple labor-intensive techniques, with face-to-face supervision by the proprietor, and with a lack of division of labor and a routinized production line. The twelve one-time Type II entrepreneurs overlap with the occupational groups in table 14, including eight former employees, whose characteristics, such as a lack of success, they approximate.

Although the transition from Type II entrepreneur is not abrupt, and merely involves the expansion of an existing firm, only three of the twelve sometime Type II entrepreneurs have made the shift. The movement (e.g., from four workers and simple tools to twenty workers with a mechanical production line) involves a major adjustment that many entrepreneurs cannot make successfully, at least without some additional training in technique, management, and/or marketing. To leap over the threshold, the entrepreneur may have to change from face-to-face supervision of workers to the delegation of responsibility to submanagers or foremen; from assigning one worker several steps in the operation to designating specialized work tasks in a mass-production line; and from direct consumer sales to the development of regular wholesale buyers. In addition, the entrepreneur may need to borrow additional funds, unless retained earnings from his previous operations have been high. Frequently, economies of scale result if an enterprise produces at least the minimum rate of output needed to develop an assembly line and sell regularly to wholesale buyers. However, achieving a rate of output above the threshold for a sustained period may require simultaneous increments in orders, financing, employment, materials quotas, and in some cases, skills—a difficult task, as illustrated below by the case of Mr. Krishnamurty.

As in James McCrory's study of manufacturing entrepreneurs in 1955 in the Punjab, the obstacles to the growth of Type II firms are not a lack of diligence, determination, resourcefulness, or thrift on the part of the entrepreneurs.[6] Instead, the barriers to expansion of these enterprises are explainable partly in terms of their weakness and vulnerability in an economy with a high degree of concentration of power (by government and foreign enterprises, and large indigenous business houses) and partly by a policy with few effective measures to lessen the concentration. In 1969/70, the median asset level of the firms of sometime Type II entrepreneurs was Rs. 22,000. In 1958, 97.3 percent of the assets of companies in India were held by companies with assets of one million rupees or more.[7] Despite the breakup of the managing agency system since 1970, there is no evidence that the concentration of holdings has lessened.

For the entrepreneur, the lack of training in business and technical, managerial and marketing experience is perhaps one of the major barriers to success. The small-scale entrepreneur usually needs to have a minimum level of skills in production, engineering, marketing, financing, purchasing, organization, labor relations, and relationships with government, as the unit cost of acquiring high-level personnel for such a size firm may be prohibitive. Most entrepreneurs, who do not belong to the large out-of-state business families, do not have the network of relationships with business-oriented friends and relatives to obtain access to trustworthy management personnel or even to acquire a reliable evaluation of the ability and integrity of prospective managers. In addition, those with greater experience in business have more time to acquire retained earnings to increase the capital available for their initial venture in manufacturing.[8] Thus as tables 15 and 16 indicate, there is a significant positive relationship between the experience of the respondent in entrepreneurial and managerial positions (outside agriculture) and the success of the entrepreneur.

The median age of the entrepreneurs (on 1 January 1971) was forty-three, relatively young when compared to studies of Michigan and Philippine entrepreneurs, who were involved in larger firms.[9] Older entrepreneurs, with more time to acquire business experience, are slightly more successful than younger enterpreneurs (table 17). The three entrepreneurs less than forty with incomes more than Rs. 25,000 in 1969/70 were directing enterprises which were closely related to their fathers' business empires or which drew heavily from their fathers for capital and connections.

TABLE 15
Management and Entrepreneurial Experience
and Income Class of Entrepreneur

1969/70 Income Class of Entrepreneur (rupees per annum)	Years of Experience in Nonagricultural Business			
	1–10	11–20	21–30	31–50
2,500 and below	6	4	1	0
2,501–10,000	4	8	2	0
10,001–50,000	5	6	6	0
Above 50,000	1	1	7	0
Not available	1	3	2	1

NOTE: Where Y is net income class (as indicated in table 11) and X is the number of years of experience of the major entrepreneur, $Y = 2.88302 + 0.089694X$, $t = 2.48273$, and the regression coefficient is significant at the 2 percent level.

TABLE 16

Years of Management and Entrepreneurial
Experience and Value Added of Firm

1969/70 Gross Value Added of Firm (rupees per annum)	Years of Experience in Nonagricultural Business			
	1–10	11–20	21–30	31–50
0–24,999	7	10	1	0
25,000–99,999	4	7	4	1
100,000 & above	4	3	10	0
Not available	0	2	2	0

NOTE: Where Y is 1969/70 gross value added and X is the number of years of experience of the major entrepreneur, $Y = -53670.37500 + 15114.00781X$, $t = 2.14681$, and the regression coefficient is significant at the 5 percent level.

TABLE 17

Age and Income Class of Entrepreneur

1969/70 Income Class of Entrepreneur (rupees per annum)	Age of Entrepreneur				
	20–29	30–39	40–49	50–59	60–69
2,500 or less	2	5	3	0	1
2,501–10,000	0	4	8	2	0
10,001–50,000	0	6	9	1	0
Above 50,000	1	0	3	3	1
Not available	0	0	2	0	3

TRAINING AND EDUCATION

An important determinant of the rate of industrial growth is the rate at which the techniques available to developed industrial areas and entrepreneurs are transferred and dispersed to prospective industrial areas and entrepreneurs. Some of the ways these technical skills become embodied in prospective entrepreneurs are through employment, training, and education. The largest number of entrepreneurs (twenty-eight) received their technical knowledge from a position in another firm within the industry. Eleven of the entrepreneurs, five of whom had been employed in a previous firm in the same industry, acquired some technical expertness in training programs (table 18)—

TABLE 18
Sources of Technical Experience and Expertness
of Entrepreneurs

Source	Foreign	Domestic
Employment in the same industry	2	26[a]
Formal training programs	1	8
Informal training programs	2	[b]
Partnership or collaboration with experienced persons	1	5
Engineering education	0	6
Assistance from spouse's relatives	0	3
Assistance from a major buyer	1	0
TOTAL	7	48

NOTE: The fifty-five responses came from forty-two entrepreneurs, as some entrepreneurs received technical help from more than one source.
a. Eight of the respondents were employed in a family firm.
b. Domestic informal training is too difficult to count. It is of interest to indicate the number of entrepreneurs who received informal training from businessmen abroad.

from a local technical training institute (with a one-year course), from firms, and from the government's National Small Industries Corporation.

In six instances, the person committing his capital collaborated or formed a partnership with someone with expertness in the industry. C. V. Shah, who started as an agent and later a partner with a Danish businessman in India in the bottling and distribution of natural gas and the import of gas equipment, eventually moved into the production, bottling, and distribution of liquid-petroleum gas, and manufacture of gas ranges and stoves throughout much of India. The family of V. L. Das, with wide access to finances and experience in manufacturing joined with the Lakotia family, less experienced and less wealthy but with a background in flour milling, to establish 20 flour mills throughout India. Three entrepreneurs married into families with experience relevant for the business. Also, one entrepreneur, S. L. Gupta, was provided with the technical knowledge in Calcutta (and in Vizag) for the manufacture of steel drums and galvanized products by a major customer, an Indian-American–owned petroleum company, which was restricted by the Indian government in the amount of vertical expansion of production it could undertake.

Six of the fifty-four entrepreneurs in Vizag, primarily a city with light industry, are graduate engineers (have a bachelor's degree in engineering or have passed examinations qualifying them to become an associate member of the Institute of Engineers, A.M.I.E.), a proportion lower than the twelve of fifty-two in Berna's 1957 sample of entrepreneurs in Madras and Coimbatore, Tamil Nadu, important centers for machinery, electric motor, and tractor trailer production. The relatively large number of engineers in entrepreneurial activity is accounted for by the large post-independence output of graduate engineers and their relatively low average salary and high rate of unemployment. Indicators of business success place Vizag engineers near the sample median. An engineering education helped to compensate, in part, for the lack of opportunity to learn the technical aspects of the business in a relative's firm, since only one of the fathers had been in business (in an unrelated industry).

Only two of the entrepreneurs had a university education in commerce or business administration. Their success was no higher than the sample median. This was true, not so much because of the orientation of university departments of commerce and business administration toward managerial and administrative positions rather than entrepreneurial activity, but because of a negative selectivity factor. University graduates in business rarely undertake entrepreneurial activity in the small-scale sector unless they have been "pushed" into it as a result of a lack of success as managers of larger firms or because of low alternative salaries.

Employment in the industry and formal training and education frequently were not adequate for the entrepreneur to master the process essential for a complex production line. Training and education were often narrowly oriented, and not geared toward practical learning. Entrepreneurs with no or inadequate education, training, and experience could, however, in some industries start a very small firm with only a few employees and, with the accumulation of experience, reading, and short training courses, expand the firm in a gradual fashion as the appropriate skill was mastered.

The median educational level of the entrepreneurs, who are all male, is some university, which is extremely high when compared to that of the male population of Vizag District urban areas, 63 percent of whom have not completed primary school. Furthermore, 46 percent of the sample are college graduates compared to 3 percent for this population group in Vizag. The median educational level of the Vizag entrepreneur is substantially above the medians for industrial entrepreneurs in Nigeria and even Michigan where the medians for firm employment size are higher than in Vizag (table 19).[10]

The high educational level of Vizag industrialists compared to that of Nigerian industrialists results in part from the higher percentage of the school-age population enrolled in educational institutions in India, a relative difference which widens substantially as the comparison moves toward higher levels of education (table 20). One of the effects of the earlier and further advancement of education in India is that the supply of positions for graduates in the government service and white-collar occupations is greater (relative to the population) in Nigeria than in India, an observation consistent with the fact that Nigeria has not yet encountered the high rate of unemployment among university graduates that India faces. Thus, the Nigerian educated person is less likely than his Indian counterpart to be "pushed" into entrepreneurial activity. Although cross-cultural comparability is not precise, studies indicate the ratio of the salaries of government officers to business executives (both in "higher posts") is 1.06:1 in India and 2.50:1 in Nigeria. Elsewhere I have shown that one would expect hired business executives and self-employed entrepreneurs in the same post to receive comparable *salary* earnings. If risk premiums and returns to capital for the entrepreneur are excluded (rates which are not likely to vary substantially between India and Nigeria), it seems likely that the salary of government officials relative to the salary (i.e., implicit or explicit labor and management earnings) of the self-employed entrepreneur is higher in Nigeria than in India. Thus, the high level of educational attainment of Indian entrepreneurs is partly a result of the limited options available to graduates in government service and in the private sector.[11]

The higher educational level of Vizag entrepreneurs than of Nigerian and United States entrepreneurs is partly due to the greater importance of relations with the public bureaucracy in India. The Indian industrialist, faced by the necessity of obtaining quotas and licenses, is more dependent upon government for the success of his firm than the entrepreneur in the *medium-sized* manufacturing plant in the Michigan sample. (The large U.S. industrial corporation, of course, is much more dependent upon the favor of the government than the medium-

TABLE 19
Distribution of Educational Attainment of Selected Entrepreneurs and Populations

Educational Level	Vizag Entrepreneurs (1971) (%)	Vizag District Males[a] (%)	Nigerian Industrial Entrepreneurs (1965)[b] (%)	Michigan Industrial Entrepreneurs (1960–1962)[c] (%)	American Big Business Leaders (1952)[c] (%)	Population of Michigan[c,d] (%)
Less than secondary graduate	17	85	85	36	13	59
Secondary graduate	28	12[e]	8	25	11	26
Some college or university	9	0	3	19	19	8
College or university graduate	46	3	4	20	57	7
TOTAL	100	100	100	100	100	100

a. *Census 1961*, Handbook, Vizag District, pp. 328–329; comprises males five years and older in Vizag District's urban areas.

b. Harris, "Nigerian Entrepreneurship," p. 343. The sample included primarily private entrepreneurs with more than ten employees in Nigeria in sawmilling, furniture making, rubber processing, printing, garment making, baking, and others. The median employment size of the firm is a little above that of the Vizag sample.

c. Collins, Moore, and Unwalla, *The Enterprising Man*, p. 237. The industrial entrepreneurs include a sample of those in manufacturing from six industrial areas in lower Michigan. The median employment size of the firms is substantially higher than in the Visakhapatnam sample. Big business leaders are primarily large corporate executives taken from a study by W. Lloyd Warner and James C. Abegglen, in which the firms are even much larger in terms of employment size than those in the Michigan sample.

d. The population of Michigan is taken from the 1960 census and comprises individuals twenty-five years and older.

e. Data on persons who are only secondary graduates and those who have some college or university are not separated.

TABLE 20
Literacy and Educational Enrollment in the United States, India, and Nigeria

Indicator	United States	India	Nigeria
Primary enrollment rates[a]	70 (1963)	38 (1962)	31 (1963)
Secondary enrollment rates[b]	109 (1963)	31 (1962)	6 (1963)
Decile ranking (primary and secondary rates combined)[c]	I (1960) (top decile)	VIII (1959)	VIII (1960)
Higher education enrollment rates (denominator—total population)[d]	2.577 (1964)	0.284 (1963)	0.014 (1964)
Decile ranking[e]	I (1960)	VI (1959)	X (1960)
Literacy rates[f]	98.5 (1959)	42.3 (1961)	NA[g]
Decile ranking[h]	II (1959)	VIII (1951)	IX (1952)

SOURCES: United Nations, *Compendium of Social Statistics: 1967* (New York, 1968). Bruce M. Russet; Hayward Alker, Jr.; Karl W. Deutsch; Harold D. Lasswell; et al., *World Handbook of Political and Social Indicators* (New Haven: Yale University Press, 1964).

a. Primary school enrollment as a percentage of the population aged five to fourteen years. Concepts of what a primary education is are not strictly comparable, nor does the five- to fourteen-year-old age group always correspond to the expected years of primary attendance. For example, the higher rate for secondary enrollment than for primary enrollment in the United States is a reflection of a lack of coincidence between primary school years and the age range, five to fourteen. *Compendium,* pp. 353–356.

b. Secondary school enrollment as a percentage of the population aged fifteen to nineteen years. *Compendium,* pp. 353–356.

c. Country decile rankings (i.e., I–X) for primary and secondary school pupils as a percentage of the population aged five to nineteen. Russet et al., *Handbook,* pp. 213, 218–220.

d. Enrollment in higher education (postsecondary school, including universities, teachers' colleges, professional schools, etc.) as a percentage of the total population. Because of the large age range for students in higher education, total population was selected as a denominator, rather than a particular age group. *Compendium,* pp. 304, 370–371.

e. Country decile rankings for students enrolled in higher education as a percentage of the total population. Russet et al., *Handbook,* pp. 213–216.

f. Literacy indicates the ability to read *and* write a simple message (in any language). *Compendium,* pp. 319, 323.

g. Not available around 1960.

h. Country decile rankings for the number of literate persons as a percentage of the population aged fifteen and over.

sized U.S. firm, which would be considered large in the Indian context.) The greater emphasis upon controls in the Indian economy
places more premium upon the art of persuasion, a skill enhanced by
education, and upon obtaining influence, which is highly correlated
with income and education.

Tables 21 and 22 indicate a positive relationship between educational attainment and the success of the major entrepreneur. Persons with
more education would be expected to have a larger body of knowledge
available for making decisions. In addition, the verbal skills of the
better-educated person would assist him in acquiring new ideas and
methods, corresponding and conversing in business relationships,
understanding instruction manuals and other routine information,
and relating to the government bureaucracy. Finally, the mathemati-
cal ability of the entrepreneur with more education should facilitate
the computation of transactions and the use of records as an instru-
ment in firm analysis. Since some of the knowledge and skill acquired

TABLE 21
Education and Income Class of Entrepreneur

| Education Completed | 1969/70 Income Class (rupees per annum) | | | |
	2,500 & less	2,501– 10,000	10,001– 50,000	Above 50,000
Primary	4	2	2	0
Secondary	1	8	4	2
University	5	3	9	6

TABLE 22
Education of Enterpreneur and Value Added of Firm

Education Completed	0–24,999	25,000– 99,999	100,000 & above	Not Available
Primary	6	1	1	1
Secondary	5	8	4	1
University	6	8	11	0

NOTE: Where Y is 1969/70 gross-valued added (in rupees per annum), X_1 is the entrepreneur's educational achievement (as indicated in table 12, X_2 is the entrepreneur's
age, $Y = 36.7982 + 0.1938X_1 + 0.0754X_2$, $t_1 = 2.2238$, and the multiple regression coefficient on X_1 is significant at the 5 percent level.

in school would be helpful in entrepreneurial activity, educational attainment would be expected to be positively related to entrepreneurial supply and success.[12]

Education is one of the intermediate variables which account for the higher level of entrepreneurial success by those with a higher socioeconomic background. As indicated previously, Hindu twice-born entrepreneurs have a higher median educational attainment than other entrepreneurs, a reflection of a positive correlation between education and caste ranking in the Vizag population as a whole.[13] Out-of-state entrepreneurs have a median educational level (a bachelor's degree) that is higher than that of in-state entrepreneurs (secondary to some university) (table 6). Because of the costs of and barriers to movement and the high premium placed upon the link-language, English, entrepreneurs from out-of-state can be considered a select group. In addition, because the levels of education and industrialization are lower in Vizag than in northern cities such as Calcutta, Delhi, and Ferozabad, Vizag has a smaller class of educated industrialists. Finally, part of the relationship between education and entrepreneurial success results from the fact that education is positively correlated to variables directly related to paternal economic status, such as initial capital.

THE ACQUISITION OF CAPITAL

Entrepreneurs in single small-scale enterprises have not usually had access to funds from organized financial institutions, at least prior to bank reorganization and nationalization in July 1969. In addition, the social sanctions and networks of relationships in Indian society usually were not sufficient to make the prospective lender or partner feel secure in advancing funds to a person who was not a close relative, of the same caste, or linked with the lender in a customary patron-client relationship. Thus, raising the initial capital of the firm was a major barrier to entry. Even the smallest industrial enterprise may require Rs. 5,000–10,000, equivalent to a few years' earnings for prospective entrepreneurs with a median income.

The extended family, because of its age composition and size, may be able to mobilize funds that the prospective entrepreneur (median age of entry into sample firms thirty-five) would not have available. Sixty-one percent of the entrepreneurs (thirty-three of fifty-four) indicated that a part of the initial capital for the firm was raised from other members of the family (ancestors, siblings, descendants, and spouses). Forty-four percent (twenty-four) received most or all of their initial capital from the family (table 23). The figure for at least partial assistance from the family is greater (74 percent), if you consider capital raised for the entrepreneur's initial business venture (which may not necessarily have been the sample firm). Even though Vizag entrepreneurs are very dependent upon the family for initial funds, they are slightly less dependent on the family than participants in my sample of Nigerian entrepreneurs (from the same size of firms). Fifty-four percent of these entrepreneurs received most or all of their initial capital from the family. However, only 71 percent of the Nigerian sample received at least part of their initial capital for their first enterprise from the family.[14]

Very often the major contributors of initial capital to the chief entrepreneur are close relatives who become partners in the enterprise. There is a significant positive relationship between initial share capital and the number of relatives of the major entrepreneur in the firm.[15]

The family economic status of the entrepreneur is a crucial factor affecting the availability of capital for new industrial enterprises, and thus the supply and success of industrial entrepreneurs. Entrepreneurs with high parental economic status had a median initial capital of Rs. 167,000, compared to Rs. 35,000 for those with low or medium economic status (table 23).[16] It is reasonable to assume that this relationship between parental economic status and initial capital is the tip of the iceberg whose surface depicts a positive relationship between parental economic status and entry into industrial entrepreneurship.

Those with high parental economic status received a little more initial financial support from their family. Ten of the seventeen (59 percent) with a high father's economic status received most of their funds from their family, while four additional ones received some support from this source. In comparison, only fourteen of thirty-three (42 percent) with low or medium economic status received most of their initial financial support from their family, with eight more receiving some support from it. Those who received most of their initial support from their families had a higher median capital, Rs. 70,000, than those who provided their own support, Rs. 45,000. Furthermore, major industrial families used their control of banks, prior to bank nationalization in July 1969, to fund the enterprises of their own families, relatives, and business communities. It can be conjectured that a relatively large number of prospective entrepreneurs from low or medium economic status did not become entrepreneurs because of the lack of family finances[17] (see also Appendix C).

TABLE 23
Major Sources of Initial Capital for Firms
(with median initial capital[a] in parentheses)

Source	Economic Status of Entrepreneur's Father				
	High	Medium	Low	NA[b]	Total
Personal savings of entrepreneur from previous business[c]	2 (450,000)	7 (60,000)	1 (60,000)	0	10 (60,000)
Personal savings of entrepreneur from previous employment	0	2 (3,000)	1 (4,000)	2 (100,000)	5 (4,000)
Personal savings of entrepreneur from agriculture	0	2 (15,000)	0	0	2 (15,000)
Personal savings and partner(s)' savings[d] from agriculture	1 (300,000)	1 (100,000)	0	0	2 (200,000)
Personal savings and family's savings[e] from previous business	4 (100,000)	4 (30,000)	0	1 (250,000)	9 (40,000)
Family's savings[f] from previous business	10 (133,000)	8 (50,000)	1 (90,000)	0	19 (85,000)
Family's savings[f] from previous employment	0	1 (35,000)	1 (6,000)	0	2 (20,500)
Family's savings[f] from agriculture	0	1 (200,000)	0	0	1 (200,000)
Inherited business	0	2 (21,500)	0	0	2 (21,500)
Bank loan	0	1 (45,000)	0	1 (12,000)	2 (28,500)
TOTAL	17 (167,000)	29 (35,000)	4 (33,000)	4 (100,000)	54 (45,000)

NOTE: Capital refers to equity and loan capital.

a. Measured in rupees.

b. Not available.

c. Business indicates nonagricultural or nonprofessional business.

d. Partner(s) implies a person who is not related to the entrepreneur.

e. Differentiated from the next category by the fact that the entrepreneur is responsible for more than one-half of the savings.

f. Family refers to ancestors, siblings, descendants and spouses.

SUMMARY

For most entrepreneurs and their families, a manufacturing business entailed a step-by-step progression, and not a sharp break, from less complex economic activities with which they were familiar. Among entrepreneurs whose previous occupation involved management responsibility, the largest number had been engaged in trade and sales. Former traders entered manufacturing to insure a regular source of supply, or as a result of the perception of increased opportunities for profits in industry relative to trade. The major catalyst for the shift to industry was deliberate post-independence government policy to encourage import substitution in manufacturing through higher tariffs, tighter import quotas, and an industrial policy that encouraged the use of domestic inputs.

The median education of the Visakhapatnam entrepreneur is extremely high when compared with the population of Vizag, and even substantially above the medians for industrial entrepreneurs in comparable studies in other mixed capitalist economies, such as Nigeria and the United States. This high educational attainment is attributed primarily to the limited employment options available to graduates in government service and the private sector.

The major source of initial capital and funds for training and education is the extended family. The economic status of the family of the entrepreneur is a crucial factor affecting the availability of capital for new industrial enterprises, and thus the supply and success of industrial entrepreneurs.

Some of the evidence of this chapter reinforces the findings of the previous chapter concerning the class origins and mobility of entrepreneurs, even though the questions investigated in the two chapters vary. The resources and privileges associated with high paternal economic status made available more prior management experience, more technical and management training, more education, and more initial capital—factors related to entrepreneurial success and supply. As a part of this pattern, those with little or no prior entrepreneurial and management responsibility frequently became entrepreneurs because of "push" factors such as the lack of attractive options or the threat of persistent unemployment, rather than "pull" factors, such as the prospect of high rates of profit.

See Appendix C for additional information for chapter 5.

6

THE RELATIONSHIP
TO GOVERNMENT, AND THE
LARGE-SCALE SECTOR

THE first part of this chapter examines the various types of government assistance to entrepreneurs, including some of the characteristics of the aid recipients, the nature of the programs, and the author's evaluation of them. The next section evaluates the impact of controls on entrepreneurship, recommends policies for reducing the distortion of these controls, and identifies the interest groups that benefit from them. The final section considers the vulnerability of small indigenous firms in a landscape dominated by large public and foreign establishments.

GOVERNMENT ASSISTANCE TO ENTREPRENEURS

Differential access to government assistance is a major factor related to the supply and success of entrepreneurs. Entrepreneurs with greater business experience and paternal, caste, and educational status are more likely to be successful in receiving government assistance (table 7) because they have more erudition, a more extensive network of influential acquaintances, and more resources available to acquire information. Those who receive government assistance, such as the leasing of land or buildings (primarily in the industrial estate provided by the Vizag District Department of Industries), or financial assistance have a higher degree of success than others (table 24). However, a part of the reason for this relationship is that government agencies are

TABLE 24
Government Assistance and Success of Entrepreneurs

Type of Government Assistance	Number of Entrepreneurs	Median Value Added[a] of Firms	Median Employment of Firms	Entrepreneurs Not Receiving Assistance	Median Value Added[a] of Firms Not Receiving Assistance	Median Employment of Firms Not Receiving Assistance
Lease, sale, or subsidized rental of land and/or building	27	83,000	15	27	21,000	7
Financial assistance[b]	10	133,500	15	44	40,000	12
Technical or management assistance	4	35,000	14	50	41,000	12

a. Measured in rupees per annum (in fiscal year 1969/70).
b. Does not include financial assistance from the State Bank of India.

more likely to assist entrepreneurs who are successful and show the capability of further success.

In the remainder of this section, I elaborate on and evaluate the three types of government assistance most frequently mentioned by entrepreneurs—assistance in an industrial estate, technical or management assistance, and financial assistance. Twenty-five of the twenty-seven entrepreneurs who leased land or buildings, or received subsidized rent from the government were in the industrial estate provided by the Department of Industries of Vizag District. An industrial estate is "a tract of land which is subdivided and developed according to a comprehensive plan for the use of a community of industrial enterprises."[1] The primary objective of the program of industrial estates, introduced around 1955 in India, was to assist in the development of small industry.[2] The Vizag industrial estate, a plot of about eighty acres owned by the Department of Industries, which began leasing to firms in 1960, includes a series of buildings and sites suitable for factories. Available on the estate are land and buildings for sale or long-term lease to industrial units, a common service facility used as a general engineering workshop and repair unit, offices of the Department of Industries with personnel who can provide limited technical and management assistance, and essential services such as roads, water, electricity, drainage, and telephone.

One of the advantages of the estate from the standpoint of the entrepreneurs is its convenient location with regard to transportation links (railways, airlines, and major roads), markets, sources of supply, and service and repair shops. Although in practice very few firms use the Department of Industries' workshops, because insufficient funds, supervision, and maintenance of the shop limit the scope of the services, many of the entrepreneurs get fabrication, structural, and repair work done at some of the private engineering workshops on the estate. In some instances, financial assistance can be arranged by the Department of Industries, especially concessions on rent in the first three to five years of the enterprise.

In the evaluation of programs to aid private entrepreneurs, I start with the premise that the programs should pay for themselves in the long run, unless the programs create positive spillover effects or redistribute income in a clearly desirable way. A program that does not pay for itself, that is, where the recipient of the service is not charged an economic price, involves a subsidy to him. Since the alternative to a subsidy is the allocation of resources for other investment or consumption purposes, the burden of proof for a subsidy should fall on its advocate. One justification for subsidies is an instance where there are spillovers, or external economies (as defined in the broader sense by development economists such as Scitovsky), that is, where social profitability of a project exceeds its commercial profitability as a result of divergences between money receipts and real benefits to society, and between money costs and social costs. However, since the "external economies" argument is convenient for planners to use to support projects that are economically untenable but politically favored, it is essential that the nature of the positive divergences be made explicit.[3] In my view, another justification for subsidies to a program or project might be to improve the distribution of income. This principle would be consistent with, for instance, subsidies to distribute rice or milk to low-income families, but not to provide automobile allowances for senior civil servants, where benefits would accrue primarily to those in the higher-income brackets.

The first program to assess is the leasing, sale, or subsidized rental of land or buildings on the industrial estate. It is difficult to object to the sale or leasing of property at full economic cost. In principle, the industrial estate may even be able to outrival other sellers and leasers of real property because of superior economies of location, and agglomerations of basic services. In practice, however, industrial estates, especially in India, tend to acquire land and construct buildings beyond a point where they can break even in the long run.[4] Where subsidization of industrial units occurs beyond this point, questions about the policy of the Department of Industries arise.

The institution of rent subsidies does increase, at the margin, the number of firms and their profitability. The analysis in chapter 4 indicates that a disproportionate number of entrepreneurs in small-scale industry in Visakhapatnam are from families with a high economic status and high caste standing. Businessmen in the industrial estate have an even higher economic and caste standing than those outside the estate. Thus, the policies of rent concessions and subsidies to industrialists in the estate tend to benefit persons with a high socioeconomic status.

Nor can the rent concessions be justified on the basis of the creation of positive spillovers above those from alternative projects. The contribution of spillovers, such as the development of human skills or the creation of forward and backward linkages, is limited because of the straitjacket placed on the expansion of production on the part of skilled and innovative entrepreneurs by the licensing of inputs discussed below.

In response to questions about technical and management advice, only four entrepreneurs mentioned the assistance of the department. One mentioned some general advice from the industrial estate engineer, another assistance to obtain an ancillary relationship and technical help from a large corporation in the city, and two an indication of agencies that could give technical assistance. In fairness, it needs to be pointed out that the department's staff is small, and not adequate for giving advice to a wide range of manufacturing industries. The department did supply routine extension information, and also assisted in liaison with loan agencies that provided technical and management assistance, such as the National Small Industries Corporation Limited.

The entrepreneurs received little benefit from the program of the Department of Industries to provide technical and management advice. Although the technical staff satisfied the formal requirements for the position, such as education, they lacked the experience in industry essential to advise entrepreneurs on practical matters such as setting up a production line, acquiring mechanical skills, scheduling maintenance and repairs, and developing records for costs. Assume, however, that competent technical advisors are available. There is much economic rationale for extension programs which provide direct entrepreneurial and technical assistance to small firms. While the alternative wage of a person with high-level technical and management skills is too high for him to be hired by a small firm, the economic cost per firm is low, if such an individual's abilities are used as an input for thirty or forty firms in a year.

It is probably not feasible administratively to charge each industrialist who utilizes management and technical assistance from the Department of Industries, or even all the industrialists in Vizag District who are eligible for aid. Yet there are enough grounds for the program even though it may involve an implicit subsidy to those receiving the assistance. The assistance generates positive externalities such as the development of managerial, supervisory, technical, and mechanical skills in the entrepreneurs and high-level employees, and an enhancement of the abilities of these persons to transmit the skills to others.

Normally, these learned skills will benefit not only the existing firm, but some will also spill over into other endeavors.[5]

When the small industrialist expands the capacity of his firm substantially, he usually requires an upgrading of technical and entrepreneurial skills. Greater size and complexity usually demands that the firm be more management- and technical-skill intensive.

If the entrepreneur planning the expansion chooses a labor-intensive technology, he can no longer rely on supervising the production process on an ad hoc basis. The organization of the firm needs to be more complex than before, with a greater necessity for delegation of responsibility, advanced planning of work tasks, and a system of communication. The entrepreneur with a more capital-intensive technology requires further technical skill or the ability to supervise it, in addition to the obvious need for more skill to organize and coordinate increased and more specialized capital and labor. The entrepreneur is not likely to have been prepared for the technical, management, and organizational problems of the larger firm, whether it be capital intensive or labor intensive.

Because of the substantial coincidence between the need for more funds and the need for further technical and managerial skills, it is important that loan agencies for small industry coordinate their operations closely with industrial extension centers. In fact, both the lending and consulting functions would be enhanced if small industry financing and industrial extension were a part of the same center. On the one hand, the evaluation of the project by the lending agency is facilitated if it is allied with an industrial extension center. On the other hand, in many cases, the center's technical and management assistance cannot be utilized without financial assistance for the expansion of the enterprise.

Nine of the entrepreneurs indicated borrowing funds from the National Small Industries Corporation Limited (NSIC), a government agency established in 1955 to assist and promote small-scale industry, supply machines to small entrepreneurs on hire-purchase (i.e., installment credit) basis, provide advice on the purchase of machines, and arrange delivery. In some cases, it provided direct-cash loans to small-scale units. Four entrepreneurs indicated the receipt of hire-purchase loans of Rs. 25,000–500,000 from the Andhra Pradesh State Finance Corporation (SFC), in which one-half of the shares were contributed by the state government, one-fourth by the Industrial Development

Bank of India and Reserve Bank of India, and one-fourth by other individuals and financial institutions. A number of respondents have reported loans from the State Bank of India. In 1969, several banks run by state governments were incorporated into the State Bank of India. Since then, according to sample entrepreneurs, loans to small-scale industrial enterprises have increased substantially.

The interest charges and repayment terms for small industry loans by the NSIC and SFC are comparable with commercial banking standards, except for refinancing by the SFC at concessional rates. Nevertheless, like most small loans in less-developed economies, NSIC-SFC small loans are not self-financing. First, the costs of senior and junior staff for processing loan applications, enforcing agreements, and collecting repayments, in addition to overhead costs, are higher per rupee loaned than for larger loans. Second, the ratio of bad debts to loans is higher for small loans. Finally, NSIC and SFC incur substantial expenses in providing technical and management assistance to small entrepreneurs. In terms of the criteria used here for evaluating programs, there seems little reason to depart from strict banking standards to provide what are, in effect, subsidies to the small-loan recipients. Some small entrepreneurs would still be funded even if commercial standards for lending were used. Furthermore, in time, profitable establishments can generate enough retained earnings for expansion. However, there are reasons, analogous to those indicated above, for subsidizing the component of the loan agencies which provides technical and management assistance to entrepreneurs.

GOVERNMENT CONTROLS

The Indian government has tried to influence industrial investment and production by physical controls operated partially through a licensing system. The purposes of these controls are to guide and regulate production according to targets of the Five-Year Plans, to protect and encourage small industrial firms, to prevent the concentration of ownership, and to promote balanced economic development between the different regions in the country.[6]

Despite recent changes aimed at decreasing licensing restrictions for small industry, sample entrepreneurs have been hampered by inadequate quotas although, as might be expected, large firms have encountered even greater inadequacies (table 25). Among firms with a value added of less than Rs. 100,000, entrepreneurs born within the city, who are more likely to know someone involved in allocating the quota, have fewer problems in obtaining quotas. However, among the larger firms, out-of-city entrepreneurs (virtually all from large business families with substantial resources and experience for dealing with the public bureaucracy, great scope for interfirm transfers, and substantial bargaining power in location) have had less difficulty with quota constraints (table 26).

The system of awarding quotas of raw materials and other inputs at less than market-clearing prices presents certain problems to small-scale industry in Vizag.

(1) It subsidizes the acquisition of inputs of certain firms within an industry while at the same time making some of their competitors pay prices above a market-clearing rate on the "black market" or forego obtaining the input. Also, the lack of explicit criteria for the selection of firms gives rise to charges that quotas are allocated on the basis of bribery, influence, communal consideration, and loyalty to the political party in power.

TABLE 25
Quota Problems in Sample Firms by Size and Growth of Firms

Value Added and Growth of Firms[a]	Quota Problems	No Quota Problems
0–24,999 value added		
negative growth	1	0
zero growth	1	5
positive growth	2	1
25,000–99,999 value added		
negative growth	0	0
zero growth	3	0
positive growth	2	3
100,000 or more value added		
negative growth	3	0
zero growth	0	0
positive growth	1	2

Note: Included are only those firms for which data are available for the fiscal years 1964/65 and 1969/70.

a. Measures value added in rupees in fiscal year 1969/70, and growth in the value of output (in rupees per annum) of sample firms in the five-year period prior to fiscal year 1969/70.

TABLE 26
Quota Problems in Sample Firms by Size of Firm
and Birthplace of Entrepreneur

Value Added[a] of Firm and Birthplace of Entrepreneur	Quota Problems	No Quota Problems
0–24,999 value added		
in city	1	6
out of city	5	7
25,000–99,999 value added		
in city	2	4
out of city	6	5
100,000 or more value added		
in city	4	0
out of city	7	5
Not available		
in city	0	0
out of city	1	1
Total		
in city	7	10
out of city	19	18

NOTE: In-city and out-of-city designations indicate whether the entrepreneur was born within or without Visakhapatnam.
   a. Measured in rupees per annum (in fiscal year 1969/70).

(2) The tendency is to favor existing firms (with past production) in the allocation of quotas.[7] The uncertainty of acquiring inputs which may be absolute bottlenecks in production discourages the entry of new firms. The exit of inefficient firms from the industry is discouraged. A unit with access to an input license may continue to operate, even though average variable cost exceeds average revenue in manufacturing. It can still make a profit by acquiring inputs on the controlled market and selling them on the free market for a higher price. Several firms in the sample are producing enough to give the appearance of being genuine manufacturing firms, while making their profit on buying and selling controlled inputs.

(3) Entrepreneurs spend much time on unproductive activities, such as buying and selling controlled inputs. Some firms may "reject" a large proportion of controlled materials acquired, and then

TABLE 27

Quota Problems and Capacity Utilization in the Iron
and Steel Industry

Quota Problems	Number of Firms	Rates of Capacity Utilization (%) (average of the percentage rates of the firms)
Domestic and foreign inputs	2	28.4
Foreign inputs	2	33.5
Domestic inputs	6	38.6
None	6	43.1

NOTE: All firms were established before 1969.

sell the "rejected" material at a higher price on the free market. Other firms may twist controlled steel slightly, so that it can be legally sold as a different "product" not subject to controls. In addition, much attention has to be diverted to the problems of dealing with government agencies.

(4) There is a substantial underutilization of capital. On the one hand, the building of excess capacity is encouraged, as entrepreneurs believe this enhances their possibility of increasing quotas. Furthermore, firms which encounter problems in obtaining quotas of crucial inputs are not able to utilize capacity to the extent that others with no problem do, as table 27 indicates. Accordingly, the median rate of capacity utilization for one shift, as determined by the entrepreneur's perception of the rate in answer to question 32 in Appendix A, is only 47 percent.

(5) Entrepreneurs tend to inflate substantially their requests for controlled materials, expecting their allotments to be reduced by a specific percentage. This increases the difficulty of rational allocation.

(6) Entrepreneurs have an incentive to either use or sell all their stock of controlled materials in the fiscal year. In general, they believe that returning part of their quota will result in a cut in their quota the following year. Evidence from Bhagwati and Desai[8] indicates that, even where a firm cannot use a licensed input because of bureaucratic delays in its allocation, the firm's input is likely to be reduced in subsequent years.

(7) The absence of what might otherwise be a minor input may halt most of the firm's production because the application process to secure it may take several months. Bottlenecks which involve controlled products generally cannot be alleviated quickly. Frequently, the result is that a much larger inventory of equipment, materials, and spare parts is needed.

(8) Large industrial houses which are better organized and better informed and which can take advantage of economies of scale in dealing with the public bureaucracy are at an advantage relative to small firms.

(9) Entrepreneurs find it very difficult to plan because of the delay and uncertainty in obtaining quotas. R. T. Krishnamurty, proprietor of a Type II firm producing electric cables, wires, and conductors, for instance, agreed to a contract to increase production of electric cables for the state electricity board to a point where the value of output of his firm would be tripled. Although he soon obtained approval for a loan for the extra materials and machines needed, he received no response within the three months required by Rule 15 of the Registration and Licensing Undertakings Rule (1952)[9] to his application for the essential input of aluminum, which was controlled by the government. Because the free ("black") market price for aluminum was too high for profitable production, the orders from the board and the bank loans had to be cancelled. Many entrepreneurs such as Mr. Krishnamurty have ceased trying to expand; experience has taught them the difficulties of synchronizing the increase of orders, the acquisition of finance, and the allocation of input quotas. These difficulties discourage industrial entrepreneurship relative to entrepreneurship in trade and contracting, where problems of dealing with government agencies for quotas are fewer.

To encourage industrial entrepreneurship and diminish distortions and arbitrariness in the allocation of inputs, the licensing of industrial inputs should be rationalized and reduced, or even removed. The abolition of domestic industrial licensing, together with the decontrol of prices, would lessen some of the problems of small entrepreneurs mentioned previously, while enhancing the rate of industrial growth. The action would eliminate the implicit subsidy to successful applicants for input licenses, and would erase the price differential between the official and free markets. The Indian Administrative Service is too small, and lacks the specialized skills and the control of the wide range of policy instruments essential for detailed regulation of prices and physical output in the private sector. At present, the bureaucracy makes choices between applicants for input licenses without reference to notions of costs, benefits, and social profitability of alternative projects.[10] Decontrol would remove the bureaucracy from these decisions, and lessen the problem of arbitrariness in the awarding of quotas. Inefficient firms that survive only on the basis of access to controlled materials would encounter competition from potentially more efficient enterprises, which are now barred from entry because of a lack of inputs. Reliance on market-clearing prices would eliminate unproductive transactions on controlled inputs, remove the incentive to build excess capacity to obtain more quotas, rationalize requests and orders for materials, enhance the future planning of output, reduce time spent with the government bureaucracy, and diminish the advantages of large industrial houses in dealing with it.

There are several interest groups opposed to a policy of removal of industrial licensing. The size, influence, and control of segments of the bureaucracy in the Ministry for Industrial Development and Company Affairs, the Ministry of Industry and Supply, the Industrial Licensing Committee, and the Industrial Ministries of the states are dependent upon input quota schemes. Futhermore, leading politicians and businessmen, supported by most elements of the Indian Left, legitimize industrial licensing as being more consistent with the egalitarian and antimonopolist positions of a society attempting to construct "a socialist pattern." Thus, substantial change in licensing policy is not likely to be considered.

This, of course, is not intended to be a comprehensive discussion of the advantages and disadvantages of the decontrol of domestic inputs, but a discussion primarily from the standpoint of the facilitation of the development of industrial entrepreneurship. A number of thorough treatments of the question have been published. The most highly recommended source, although a little dated, is Bhagwati and Desai, *India: Planning for Industrialization—Industrialization and Trade Policies Since 1951.*

RELATIONSHIP TO THE LARGE INDUSTRIAL SECTOR

In 1971, the firms classified as large-scale manufacturing enterprises in Vizag were a ship-building enterprise, an oil refinery, a fertilizer plant, a heavy-plate-and-vessel establishment, a polystyrene firm, an oxygen company, a steel plant, and an electrical equipment producer (the last two of which were indigenous private firms). In addition, the port trust and the naval base had a major impact on the Vizag economy. The Government of India, through its licensing power, has blocked a number of large firms, especially foreign enterprises, from vertical expansion in order to encourage ancillary industries. A substantial share of the sample entrepreneurs established their firms with the hope of at some point becoming a supplier to one of the large enterprises that dominate the local economy.

Representatives from the large enterprises indicated a disappointment with the quality and regularity of ancillary suppliers and frequently changed them. On the other hand, entrepreneurs from small firms not associated with large industrial families complain about their vulnerability in relationship to the large-scale sector and their lack of bargaining power with large firms. They indicate that their poor quality of production frequently results partly from a lack of time available to develop the expertness in fulfilling the exact specification required by large enterprises. In addition, government policy on quotas may prevent the firm from responding soon enough to fill the orders of the large enterprises. However, in some cases representatives of large enterprises, required by government to buy from small-scale firms, assist the entrepreneur in setting up the plant, obtaining the technical skill, and even supporting the application for controlled materials.

The high dependence of sample firms upon markets from the large enterprises is indicated by the fact that twelve firms sell 50 percent or more of their output to one buyer, and an additional six firms sell at least 25 but less than 50 percent of their output to one buyer. Examples of ancillary production of sample firms include steel and machine parts, engineering products, wire, nonferrous castings, conductor cables, gaskets, valves, steel drums, pipe fittings, and bearings. Ten of the twenty sample firms in the iron and steel industry, which includes general engineering and fabrication works, in addition to iron and steel products, sell at least 25 percent of their output to a single firm—primarily the shipyard, public works department, oil refinery, port, naval base, electricity board, and a hospital. Firms dependent upon only a few buyers have risked market vulnerability in order to obtain a greater output and value added for the short run. Median value added for the firms with 25 percent or more sold to one purchaser is Rs. 65,000, compared to Rs. 40,500 for the sample as a whole. Nevertheless, one cost of the vulnerability to cutbacks in orders from a dominant customer may be frequent periods of low capacity utilization. Median capacity utilization for the ten iron and steel firms with at least 25 percent sold to one customer is 29.3 percent compared to 41.2 percent for the other ten. However, those entrepreneurs from firms with 25 or more percent of sales to one buyer are not significantly different from the sample in terms of socioeconomic background.

One example of an ancillary firm is Gupta Steel Products, which had provided galvanized steel products for an Indian-American-owned oil company in Calcutta and was given a contract in 1967 to produce oil drums for the same company in Vizag. The container company, which has the third-largest value added of sample firms, sells all its output to the refinery. Management personnel at the container company do not feel their firm is insecure, and those at the oil refinery are pleased to have an ancillary enterprise that is satisfactory and reliable.

Another firm, Andhra Containers, a producer of kerosene tins, was among the largest firms in the sample in 1964/65. However, in 1969/70 the firm was producing only one-tenth the value of output of 1964/65, and making substantial losses instead of high profits. The main reason for the decline in output was that the local oil refinery found a cheaper source of tins.

SUMMARY

Entrepreneurs with a greater paternal, caste, and educational status are more likely to be successful in receiving government assistance. Because of the lack of positive spillovers or redistributive effects, there seems little reason to subsidize two of the major schemes for small-scale entrepreneurs, the industrial estates and the loan agencies. However, programs of technical and management assistance do generate enough positive externalities, such as the creation of skills, to warrant their establishment even if they do not pay for themselves.

The Indian government has tried to direct industrial investment and output by controls operated largely through an exhaustive licensing system for materials. The awarding of licenses to entrepreneurs at controlled prices subsidizes the successful applicant and penalizes the unsuccessful one, encourages the construction of excess capacity, discourages the entry and exit of firms in the industry, distorts the allocation and use of inputs, favors the large industrial houses, and hampers the advanced planning of production. To encourage entrepreneurship and rationalize production, the author recommends the reduction or abolition of licensing.

Many entrepreneurs in sample firms are very vulnerable as a result of a high dependence upon markets from the large public and foreign enterprises.

7

CONCLUSION

In Visakhapatnam, a highly disproportionate number of entrepreneurs (especially successful ones) are from high castes and families with a high socioeconomic status. Members of the dominant castes, classes, and families can avert the threat of democratization and industrialization to their economic standing by using the advantages of wealth and position to obtain favorable concessions in jobs and businesses, to acquire appropriate work and management experience, and to invest in education, training, and industrial plant and equipment. Evidence from other studies tends to suggest that the socioeconomic status of South Asian industrial entrepreneurs is generally high.[1]

Since it is widely held that the rigidity of the Indian social structure is unique,[2] it might be argued that the high socioeconomic origins of entrepreneurs are not representative of the rest of the nonsocialist world. Yet cross-cultural studies suggest that the caste and class structure of India is fairly similar in operation to that of the southern United States and some other developed economies.[3]

The evidence of empirical studies from a wide range of social systems supports the view that the class and family origins of industrialists are much higher than that of the general population. The proportion of fathers of Filipino manufacturing entrepreneurs from an upper socioeconomic position was thirty-six times that of the popula-

TABLE 28
Occupation or Economic Sector of Fathers of Industrialists

	Nigeria 1965	
Occupational Category	Major Occupation of Fathers of Industrialists (%)	Primary Occupations of Nigerian Males, 1952–53 Census (%)
Agriculture, forestry, animal husbandry, fishing and hunting	44	79
Craftsmen, skilled and semiskilled workers engaged in producing articles	21	6
Traders and employees engaged in commerce	22	6
All government and professional workers	10	3
Other occupations	3	7
TOTAL	100	101[a]

	Greece ca. 1961	
Economic Occupational Activity	Major Activities of Fathers of Industrialists (%)	Working Population, early 1950s (%)
Craftsman	17	8
Big merchant	16	1
Small merchant	13	4
Industrialist	34	[b]
Professional man	3	1
Business executive	1	[b]
Farmer	11	50
Other activities	5	36[c]
TOTAL	100	100

TABLE 28 (continued)

United States (Michigan) 1960–1962

Occupation	Major Occupation of Fathers of Industrialists	Employed Labor Force 1940
Unskilled or semiskilled worker (including farm worker)	18	44
Skilled worker	12	11
Farmer or farm manager	19	11
Clerk, salesman, and kindred worker	6	17
Businessman, executive, manager, and official	28	8
Professional worker	10	7
Other	6	1
TOTAL	99[a]	99[a]

SOURCES: Harris, "Nigerian Entrepreneurship," p. 335; Nigeria, Federal Republic of, *Annual Abstract of Statistics 1963* (Lagos: Office of Statistics, 1963), p. 21; A. P. Alexander, *Greek Industrialists,* pp. 45, 87; Collins, Moore, and Unwalla, *The Enterprising Man,* pp. 238–239; and U.S. Bureau of the Census, *Sixteenth Census of the United States: 1940,* vol. 3, *The Labor Force: Occupation, Industry, Employment and Increase,* 1, "U.S. Summary" (Washington: G.P.O., 1943), p. 87.

a. Columns may not add up to 100 percent because of rounding.

b. Less than 0.5 percent.

c. Consists of 13 percent white-collar worker, 12 percent blue-collar worker, 10 percent civil servant, and 1 percent miscellaneous.

tion. Opportunities for industrial enterprise were available chiefly to those who were already well established financially.[4] Similarly, in Harris' sample of Nigerian entrepreneurs, 56 percent (147 of 262) of their fathers were in the nonagricultural sector compared to 21 percent of the Nigerian male population.[5] Furthermore, in Alexander's study of Greek industrialists, 54 percent (282 of 522) of their fathers were big merchants, industrialists, professional men, or business executives compared to 2 percent of the total working population[6] (table 28). These figures support the contention that the socioeconomic class of the entrepreneurs was far above that of the population at large.

Likewise, on the basis of the scanty data available, entrepreneurs in the United States appear to have a substantially higher socioeconomic background than the population as a whole. It is true that two-thirds of the sample entrepreneurs in Michigan studied by Collins, Moore, and Unwalla described their early family life as "poor" or "under-privileged." But the only other choices were "affluent" or "well off."[7] Given the lack of any choice corresponding to a middle-level category, respondents may have avoided designations implying higher incomes. Furthermore, entrepreneurs may have evaluated parental family income in terms of contemporary standards (the 1960s) and in comparison with their own high level of economic well being. The vast underrepresentation of Michigan sample fathers in unskilled, semiskilled, clerical, sales, and kindred work (24 percent from the sample and 61 percent from the general labor force), together with the disproportionate representation of fathers in business, executive, managerial, and official, farm owner and managerial, and professional work (57 percent compared to 26 percent), points to median incomes substantially above the corresponding population of their period (table 28).[8]

Executives in large corporations, who as a group enjoy higher remuneration and lower risk, are likely to originate from an economically more select portion of the population than medium-scale industrial entrepreneurs.[9] The U.S. business elite in 1952 was comprised largely of "the sons of men of relatively high occupational status, the sons of business and professional men." Among the fathers of this elite, the number of executives or owners of larger businesses was eight times its proportion within the general population, while the number of unskilled or semiskilled laborers was one-sixth its percentage in the population.[10] In terms of socioreligious communities and the business establishment, there are rough parallels between Protestants of northern and western European origin in the United States and Hindu twice-born castes in India, and between black Americans and Indian untouchables.[11]

In the Soviet Union in 1936, the latest date for reliable information on parental occupational origins, the sons of white-collar employees, professionals, or business owners had six times the representation of the sons of manual workers and farmers in industrial executive positions. This occurred despite the revolution of 1917 which overturned the existing class structure.[12]

Entrepreneurs in Nigeria, Greece, and Michigan underwent, in the aggregate, an intergenerational upward movement (i.e., from father to son) in occupational status and material level of living.[13] However, the fact that the socioeconomic status of the entrepreneurs was higher than that of their fathers does not conflict with the evidence that the paternal economic status of entrepreneurs was higher than that of the population as a whole.[14] Essentially, the socioeconomic status of the entrepreneurs was higher than the status of their fathers, which was substantially higher than that of the general population.

The foregoing discussion should make clear that the heroic model of the entrepreneur presented by previous empirical studies resulted from the types of questions posed to the informants. Although the data indicating the upward social and economic mobility of industrialists are useful, this exclusive focus detracts from the considerable contrast between the socioeconomic class background of entrepreneurs and that of the general population.[15]

The findings here suggest that the socioeconomic class status of businessmen is substantially higher than the general population in mixed and capitalist economies (and perhaps even in socialist economies). Industrial business activity, rather than being a path for substantial upward socioeconomic mobility, is a way of maintaining or defending privileged status, and enhancing or consolidating the high economic position of the family.

Several questions arise out of the findings of this study which have implications for the future study of entrepreneurship. More research is needed to test whether the high socioeconomic status of entrepreneurs is as widespread as existing empirical studies seem to suggest. One major deficiency in the studies available is the lack of temporal perspective on trends in the distribution of the class origins of entrepreneurs. One key question to investigate is whether the socioeconomic status of industrialists has increased or decreased over what it was earlier, for instance, one or two decades ago.[16]

One challenge arising from my findings would be to try to find geographical areas or industrial sectors where a disproportionate number of entrepreneurs have a low class or caste background, and to explain how these entrepreneurs were able to surmount the types of barriers usually encountered by persons of low economic status. Even where one may not be able to find overall disproportionate representation of lower-status persons in business activity, it might be possible to study a few individual entrepreneurs of low socioeconomic background to attempt to find reasons for their success. In India, especially, it would be of interest to identify strategies that families, communities, or castes have used to achieve upward mobility to success in business.

There are a number of important policy questions that require more study. Research is needed to recommend measures that governments can undertake, especially in their programs for entrepreneurial development and industrial extension, to increase the participation of those from a low socioeconomic background in business ventures. Scholars might also examine whether steps can be taken to induce financial institutions to contribute to a redistribution of opportunities for business ventures. The effect of widespread government regulations and controls on the availability of economic opportunities for the "weaker segments" of the population is another question to be investigated. In addition, existing programs on the part of Indian official agencies, such as concessions to economically "backward" castes, inducements to locate industries in economically "backward" areas, and the promotion of small-scale industry, need to be evaluated for their contribution to a greater fluidity of economic classes. A further item for consideration is how these agencies can identify those with low socioeconomic status who might be potential entrepreneurs.

This study has not analyzed the indirect effect of the development of entrepreneurs on persons with low income or low status. Does the effect of the development of entrepreneurship on employment, output, and productivity increase the economic welfare of the lower classes, even though few of them may become entrepreneurs? Furthermore, scholars may want to assess the cost of an emphasis upon egalitarianism in entrepreneurial development programs in terms of the amount of economic growth foregone.

The question of the relationship of entrepreneurship to social mobility needs more analysis by sociologists and psychologists. For example, scholars in these fields might be able to identify possible obstacles in the education, training, and socialization of children from lower-class families which may impede their eventual acquisition of entrepreneurial skills and qualities. In addition, more work can be done on the extent to which low-achievement motivation is associated with and influenced by a low economic class standing.

This study has been a modest attempt to provide insights and raise questions concerning the relationship between class ranking and success and participation in entrepreneurial activity. More research is needed to enhance our understanding of the economic, social, psychological, political, and historical dimensions of this relationship, and to formulate policies to increase the opportunities for entrepreneurial activity by those with a low socioeconomic background.

Appendix A

PROCEDURES, METHODS, AND DEFINITIONS

THIS appendix elaborates on the brief statements in chapter 1 concerning the population of firms, sample of entrepreneurs, and measures of entrepreneurial success, and indicates the context of and procedures for the field research, some definitions and concepts used in the study, the interview schedule, and the letter of introduction.

From July 1970 through June 1971, I was Visiting Fulbright Professor in the Department of Economics at the postgraduate campus of Andhra University in Waltair, a suburban region within the city of Visakhapatnam, Andhra Pradesh. Because of my previous experience in organizing a field study of Nigerian manufacturing entrepreneurs, and the department's interest in research on small-scale entrepreneurs, I was asked to collaborate with Professor B. Sarveswara Rao, head of the department, in directing empirical research on Visakhapatnam (Vizag) industrialists.

As indicated in chapter 1, the universe consisted of the entrepreneurs of the fifty-eight private indigenous manufacturing establishments in Visakhapatnam listed as having five or more employees.[1] The industries which comprise this population are iron and steel (including engineering and fabrication works), cement and concrete, electrical, nonferrous metals and alloys, garments and thread, footwear, radio and electronic components, food products, wood-based industries, plastic products, printing, mineral-based industries, paper and paper products, petroleum products, and rubber and tires. Indigenous firms are those in which all the capital is Indian (i.e., firms owned by Indian citizens or agencies). "Manufacturing" involves the making of goods and articles, either by hand or with machinery. Two large-scale private enterprises established in the city between 1958 and 1970 are not included in the department's register.

The units in the register were designated as small-scale firms. A small-scale industrial unit is defined by the Ministry of Industrial Development as a unit whose capital investment (valued at the original price) in plant and machinery does not exceed Rs. 750,000. Units defined as ancillary units are classified as small scale if investment is not more than Rs. 1,000,000. There is a considerable amount of discretion in the identification of an ancillary unit. As a matter of fact, the criteria for invested capital to be designated a small-scale unit are interpreted rather liberally. If the entrepreneur thinks the state bureaucracy can help him overcome his particular difficulties more effectively than the central bureaucracy, he will use whatever means he can to gain and maintain his classification as a small-scale industrial unit.[2] This explains why eight of the entrepreneurs of these firms classified as small-scale units indicated the net worth (capital stock) of their units in January 1971 was at least Rs. 1,000,000, and why two entrepreneurs indicated an initial equity capital of at least Rs. 1,000,000.

Seventy firms remained after those outside Vizag city, established before 1958 and after 1970, and listed as having less than five employees had been eliminated from the registry of industrial units from Vizag District. The registry usually indicated the street or area where the unit was located. However, since there are no detailed maps of Vizag, in some instances the search for an establishment took as long as several hours. Five of the firms, which had registered in the hope of receiving government licenses or assistance, never commenced operation. Seven of the units were no longer operating at the time of the interview. Though seven of the twelve principals of the firms not in operation were interviewed informally, the findings were not included in the aggregated data. Data were obtained on a sample of fifty-four entrepreneurs from fifty-seven firms. (See chapter 1, note 12.)

The major indicators of the success of entrepreneurs are their income class and the gross value added of their firms. Gross value added is defined as the value of output of a firm minus purchases from other firms, and is taken from the 1969/70 fiscal year. Income refers to net

individual income from all nonagricultural and nonprofessional business endeavors from the same fiscal year. The seven income classes
were below 0, 0-2500, 2501-5000, 5001-10,000, 10,001-25,000,
25,001-50,000, and 50,000 and above. (See the interview schedule
below.) Even though the other interviewers and I could check for the
internal consistency of data, both figures on income and value added
are still subject to a margin of error. Nevertheless, information from
independent sources such as competitors, suppliers, and customers
suggests that the relative ranking of entrepreneurs and establishments
according to these indicators is not far from correct.[3]

The author, assisted by S. A. R. Sastry and/or M. Jagadeswara
Rao, lecturers in the Department of Economics at Andhra University,
Waltair, visited all firms in the population. One of the latter two conducted the interview where Telugu was essential.[4] The interview
schedule was pretested on ten sample firms. After the schedule was
revised, the ten establishments were revisited to obtain data on questions missing from the pilot questionnaire. The revised interview
schedule shown below was administered orally in sample firms.

The following letter of introduction was mailed to the principal of
each of the fifty-eight units in the population. A copy of the letter was
available to present to the respondent, if necessary, at the time of the
interview.

ANDHRA UNIVERSITY

From
Prof. B. Sarveswara Rao, M.A., Ph.D.   Waltair,
                    (Cantab.).
Head of the Dept. of Economics.   D/19-1-1971

To

Dear Sir,

The Department of Economics, Andhra University has undertaken
a Study of Entrepreneurship in small scale Manufacture in the city of
Visakhapatnam. The main objective of the study is to investigate the

determinants of the supply and success of industrial entrepreneurs in the small scale sector, in the city of Visakhapatnam, where a number of small industries predominate. In particular, the study is designed to elicit information on

    i) the key variables which affect entrepreneurial supply and success such as socio-economic background, education, training and work experience of entrepreneurs;

   ii) the factors influencing the decisions of entrepreneurs to start industrial units;

 iii) the factors influencing the decision of entrepreneurs to expand the established units, and diversification of the products; and

 iv) the difficulties or obstacles faced by entrepreneurs in the establishment or expansion of the units.

Your industrial unit is one of those selected for purposes of our study. A schedule has been prepared and my colleagues in the Department, Mr. M. Jagadeswara Rao, Mr. S. A. R. Sastry and Dr. E. W. Nafziger, American Professor and a Specialist in Entrepreneurship will visit you for collecting the necessary information. I request you to give your full co-operation in providing the required information to my colleagues. I may assure you, in this connection, that no individual or firm will be identified by name and the data or information collected will be aggregated and used purely for purposes of Research and for no other purpose. You can therefore feel free in giving the necessary information. I hope you will spare some of your valuable time for my colleagues. I may inform you in this connection that I have received considerable encouragement from the District Authorities, for our study, especially from the Deputy Director of Industries.

                        Thanking you,

                        Yours sincerely,

                        (B. SARVESWARA RAO)

The Interview Schedule Used in Sample Firms
(with the pages of the questionnaire indicated in brackets)

ENTREPRENEURSHIP IN SMALL SCALE MANUFACTURING IN THE CITY OF VISAKHAPATNAM

A. IDENTIFICATION OF THE UNIT:

Name of the Respondent:

Name of Investigator:

Date(s) of Interview

1. Name and Address of the Unit:
2. Date of Registration as Small Scale Industry:
3. Month and Year of Establishment:
4. Month and Year of First Operation:
5. Product/Products of the Unit:
6. Plant Capacity:

    a) Initial:

    b) Present:

    c) No. of Shifts Worked (1969–70):

7. Type of ownership (Single ownership/Partnership/Co-Operative/Public limited/Private limited)
8. Has this type been the same since it was established? (Yes/No)
9. If no, what changes were made? When?
10. Does the business have production, storage and sales establishments elsewhere? If so, give the address and nature of the establishments.

INSTRUCTIONS: Please note that the respondent for these questions is the top manager. For 5, name all the major products.

[2]

B. PARTICULARS OF THE OWNER/OWNERS OF THE UNIT:

Sl. No.	Name of the owner	Year of becoming owner of this unit	Age in years	Sex M/F	Marital status	Primary occupation	Birth-place	Caste and social community	Religion
1	2	3	4	5	6	7	8	9	10
1.									
2.									
3.									
4.									

INSTRUCTIONS: Note that the respondents are the principal owner(s). Where the principal owners are not available, the top manager may be contacted. If top manager(s) are also owner(s) they must be covered in addition to the principal owners. Note that no. of dependents include wife, children, parents and others whether related or not.

[3]

Sl. No.	Name of the owner	Highest educational qualification and places of education	Training (technical or business including apprenticeship)			Work or management experience before setting up this business			Name of establishment	Participation in management (Yes/No)	If yes, date of participation in management
			Type	Period	Place	Type	Period	Place			
1	2	11	12	13	14	15	16	17	18	19	20

[4]

Sl. No.	Name of the owner	Position	If yes, nature of participation in management / Type of responsibility	Father's primary occupation	His economic status (high, medium or low)	Year of residence in Vizag city	Previous place of residence (state whether city, town or village)	Year of immigration to Vizag city	Reason for immigration	No. of dependents	Are any of your relations owners or high level personnel within the unit? (specify relationship)
1	2	21	22	23	24	25	26	27	28	29	30

C. ORIGINS OF THE UNIT:

12. Who gave you the idea about starting/acquiring ownership interest in the unit?

13. Why have you decided to go for manufacturing?

14. Why this particular industry?

15. Why did you start/acquire ownership interest in the unit in this city?

16. How much did you invest at that time? Give details:

Source/ amount	Yourself	Your family members	Partners	Friends	Comm. banks	Co-Op. societies	Govt. agencies	Others (specify)
1)								
2)								

17. How did you raise your own contribution of share or loan capital?

18. What were your considerations in choosing the initial plant size?

19. Did you receive any help in establishing this unit from official agencies? (Yes/No) If yes, indicate the agency and the nature of help received.

20. Apart from money, what other help did you receive at that time from others?

Nature of help	From whom received relation/friend	His/Her occupation or business interest	Others
1	2	3	4
1. Obtaining licences and facilities from			
a) Municipality			
b) State and Central Govts.			
2. Technical Advice			
3. Advice about Staff recruitment			
4. Advice about Management			
5. Other (Specify)			

Note: For 19, items of help will be the same as that for 20.

D. OTHER BUSINESS INTERESTS OF THE OWNER(S):

21. What were the other business units owned or managed by you at the time of establishment of this unit? Give details:

	Total investment in the business (in shares & loans)	Your investment		Participations in management (Yes/No)	If yes, nature of participation	
		By shares	By loans		Position	Type of responsibility
Nature of Business						
1	2	3	4	5	6	7

E. GROWTH AND EXPANSION OF THE UNIT:

22. Have any of the following changes taken place since the unit was established? Give details:

Sl. No.	Category of change	Nature of change	Person(s) who made the decision	Reason for the change
1	2	3	4	5
1.	Expansion of the unit's capacity			
2.	Establishment of new units or branches			
3.	Improvements in design or layout of the plant			
4.	Installation of improved machinery			
5.	Introduction of new products or activities			
6.	Changes in the product mix			
7.	Important changes in marketing arrangements			
8.	Any other changes connected with output and productivity (Specify)			

[9]

F. OTHER BUSINESS UNITS OWNED OR MANAGED AFTER THE ESTABLISHMENT OF THIS UNIT:

Name of business	Newly established or pre-existing unit expanded (N/P)	Investment By shares	By loans	Participation in management (Yes/No)	If yes, indicate position	Type	Product(s) related to this unit (Yes/No) If yes, nature of relationship	Purchases or sales transactions between the unit and these other business units — Purchases Qty. Value		Sales Qty. Value	
1	2	3	4	5	6	7	8	9	10	11	12

a) Business unit owned:

b) Business units managed without ownership interest:

Note: The respondent in this case is the principal owner. If he is not available the information may be obtained from the top manager.

[10]

G. PARTICULARS OF MANAGERS AND OTHER HIGH LEVEL PERSONNEL:

Sl. No.	Name of the person	Designation	Year of appointment	Age in years	Sex M/F	Marital status	Birth place	Caste & social community	Religion	Highest educational qualification and places
1	2	3	4	5	6	7	8	9	10	11

[11]

Sl. No.	Name of the person	Training (technical or business including apprenticeship)			Work or management experience before joining in this unit				Nature of duties	Father's primary occupation	His economic status H/M/L
		Type	Period	Place	Type	Period	Place	Name of the establishment			
1	2	12	13	14	15	16	17	18	19	20	21

[12]

Sl. No.	Name of the person	Years of residence in Vizag city	Previous place(s) of residence (State whether C/T/V)	Year of immigration to Vizag city	Reasons for immigration to Vizag city	No. of dependents	Are any of your relations owners or high-level personnel within this unit of (Specify relationship)
1	2	22	23	24	25	26	27

H. MANAGEMENT DECISIONS:

25. In 1969/70, who in the firm was finally responsible for deciding the following matters?

    a) Total Output:

    b) Product Mix:

    c) Block Capital raised (if any):

    d) Working Capital raised:

    e) Recruitment of High-level personnel (if any):

    f) Recruitment of labor:

I. MANAGEMENT TRAINING SCHEDULES:

26.

    a) Is there any provision for the training of the managers, supervisory and technical cadres of employees? (Yes/No)

    b) If yes, give details.

    c) Has the training received by your employees helped in raising the efficiency of your unit?

[14]

J. GOVT. ASSISTANCE UTILIZED AND EXPECTED:

27.

a) Have you approached the govt. for any help after the establishment of the unit? (Yes/No)
b) If yes, what agency did you approach?
c) For what purpose?
d) Was your purpose served?
e) Have you made use of the facilities provided by the govt. to your industry?

Facility	(Yes/No)	Are you satisfied?	If not, give reasons
1	2	3	4
1. Buildings			
2. Hire purchase facilities			
3. Technical advice			
4. Technical/business training			
5. Bank credit			
6. Others (Specify)			

f) What kind of assistance do you think govt. should provide to an industry like that of yours?

[15]

K. MARKETING ARRANGEMENTS:

28. What proportion of sales are to

	1969–70	
	Sales	Percentage
a) Government		
b) Directly to the public		
c) Wholesalers or distributors or retailers		
d) Your own subsidiary marketing organization		
e) Other manufacturing establishments		

Note: If data for 1969–70 are not available, ask for the latest year available.

[16]

L. DIFFICULTIES AND PROBLEMS FACED BY THE UNIT IN RECENT YEARS:

29. What have been the major difficulties faced by the unit? (Specify)

Sl. No.	Specific nature of the difficulty or the problem	Did you overcome the difficulty or solve the problem? Yes/No	If yes, how did you overcome the difficulty or solve the problem?
1	2	3	4
1. Procurement of materials			
a) Foreign			
b) Domestic			
2. Procurement of machinery, tools and spare parts			
3. Major breakdowns of the plant			

4. Repairs or maintenance of machinery
5. Procurement of working capital
6. Availability of labor
   a) Managerial
   b) Skilled labor
   c) Unskilled labor
7. Labor troubles
8. Transport
9. Supply of power and water
10. Marketing of products (seasonal demand, competition in the market—lack of sales agencies, etc.)
11. Tax problems
12. Others (Specify)

[17]

M. PLANS FOR THE FUTURE:

30. (a) Do you plan to expand the unit in future? (Yes/No)
    (b) Give reasons:
    (c) Specify your plans (if any):
    (d) Do you plan to expand or establish ancillary business?
    (e) If yes, specify:
    (f) Are you contemplating leaving the business?
    (g) If yes, for what reasons?

18

N. STATISTICS OF PRODUCTION, EMPLOYMENT, AMOUNT SPENT:

31. Please give information on Production, Employment, Amounts spent from the first year of operation:

Year	Total employ- ment	Production		Sales value	Amounts spent					Wages and salaries paid
		Quantity	Value		Purchases of materials (including fuel other than power)	Payments for power	Other purchases	Total purchases from other businesses (including govt.)		
1	2	3	4	5	6	7	8	9		10

32. (a) Your production in the year 1969–70 is . . . . Quantity . . . . Value
Assume that the price of your products remains the same, and
that you use the same plant and equipment.
How much more could you have produced (in rupee value)
in 1969–70 if you could have sold all that you produced?

(b) (i) For the production in the year, how many shifts per day did you work?
(ii) How many days per week did you work?
(iii) How many days in the year were lost as a result of labor troubles?

33. What is the total net worth of this business at present (January 1971)?

34. You have indicated ownership and management, and participation in business. Would you please indicate in which of the following classes your net personal income from all business endeavors for the latest year falls? (Put a cross against the relevant income class and indicate the year.)

Income Class

below 0
0–2,500
2,501–5,000
5,001–10,000
10,001–25,000
25,001–50,000
50,001 and above

35. What percentage of your working time do you spend in looking after your business affairs?

1. Full-time Management
2. Part-time Management
3. Other Management
4. Ownership responsibilities other than above
5. Other work

Total   100.00

INSTRUCTIONS: Note that "business" refers only to nonagricultural and nonprofessional business.

Appendix B
APPENDIX TO CHAPTER 4

THE *Varna* RANKING OF *Jati*s IN ANDHRA

EACH entrepreneur was asked his caste (and social community). (See item B. 9 in the interview schedule in Appendix A.) The eleven Brahmins and eight out-of-state Vaishyas gave their *varna*, rather than *jati*. The purpose of this portion of the appendix is to indicate what *varna* was designated for those who responded with their *jati*s. Dr. K. V. Ramana, Reader in the Department of Sociology, Andhra University, Waltair, Andhra Pradesh, assisted me in classifying the *jati*s of entrepreneurs according to *varna*. Five Rajus and four Komatis from Andhra were categorized as Kshatriyas and Vaishyas, respectively. Local agricultural *jati*s classified as Sudras, together with their frequency, were Kammas—3, Naidus—3, Telagas—2, Gavaras—1, Kapus—1, and Velamas—1. The three other in-state Sudras were members of the Kalavantula (dancing), Vodabalija (fishing and boat-making), and Sale (spinning and weaving) *jati*s. The Sudra entrepreneur from outside Andhra was an Ezhavor, a *jati* from Kerala traditionally engaged in tapping.

VIZAG ENTREPRENEURS AS INNOVATORS

In order to test whether my findings concerning the socioeconomic origins of the entrepreneurs would be any different if I used Schumpeter's concept, I identified the innovators in the fifty-seven sample firms. In line with the discussion in the second chapter, I have broadened the Schumpeterian concept to include as an innovator one who carried out "new combinations" in the coastal Andhran economy.

The extent to which sample entrepreneurs introduced new goods and new processes is very limited. C. V. Shah (a pseudonym), the principal in two of the sample establishments, adapted some of the technology of a foreign-owned company he gradually bought between 1942 and 1957. The personnel of Mr. Shah's enterprises developed a process to make use of previously unutilized natural gas in industry and the household, and devised a safety regulator for gas cylinders. New markets for liquid-petroleum gas, gas cylinders, stoves, and burners were created on both coasts in the 1950s and 1960s. T. D. Singh and his father, as a result of a transport bottleneck in their contracting enterprise in Burma, introduced the production of types of small steel crafts, barges, and motor launches new to South Asia. In 1967, the son brought in the production of medium-sized boats to coastal Andhra as an essential complement to the existing output of large ships in Vizag. Although S. M. Singh, no relation to T. D. Singh, imitated and adapted techniques available in advanced economies, he was one of the first in India to produce anodized products, builders' hardware and ladders, and architectural fittings made from aluminum, and to adapt this output to less-automated production techniques.

Several persons from sample firms, in addition to Messrs. Shah, T. Singh, and S. Singh, opened new markets in coastal Andhra. Each of thirteen different individuals from sample firms is responsible for introducing into Vizag one of the following innovations: the commercial production of ice, the first commerical printing press, the sawing of blue pine timber, the large-scale output of ladies' sandals, the daily delivery of fresh-wrapped bread, the mass production of hygienic dehydrated fruit pulp, galvanized iron buckets, corrugated sheet metal, electronic components, mosaic floor tiles, the first tire-retreading firm after the offical limitation in the supply of tires, the provision of certain manufactured ship parts, and the mass production of high quality white flour, atta and bran. Finally, one person was able to capture a new regular source of supply of graphite mined by his father-in-law's firm. No one in any of the other firms was an innovator, even if the broader definition is used.

Altogether there are seventeen Schumpeterian entrepreneurs, all of whom are included in my sample of fifty-four entrepreneurs, identified according to Knight's conception. In all instances in the sample, these innovators were associated with the establishment of a new firm in Vizag. Furthermore, in every case, the entrepreneur (and/or his family) had the responsibility for providing the initial capital for the firm.

As noted in chapter 2, an entrepreneur who carries out innovation produces at a unit cost lower than existing firms, and thus makes a profit above competitive returns to the factors of production. This is true even if the nature of the innovation is merely a "new combination" within a limited geographical area, such as coastal Andhra. Where the cost of transport of a good is high, the entrepreneur introducing a new combination in coastal Andhra receives some protection against innovators with a low unit cost of production in other regions. Partly because of government restrictions on licenses and quotas, discussed in chapter 6, there are substantial barriers to entry, and the expansion of capacity, by imitators. As a result of these barriers, supernormal profits ensuing from innovation are less likely to be wiped out.

Appendix C
APPENDIX TO CHAPTER 5

K. J. CHRISTOPHER, in his study of sixty-one small industrial entrepreneurs in the largest urban agglomeration in Andhra Pradesh, Hyderabad, indicated that his "findings disproved the commonly held notion that it was only moneyed people who started industries. In fact, the findings showed that availability of money was among the least important reasons for starting an industrial unit."[1] However, the sample of entrepreneurs interviewed was limited to those who had already survived to the point of "continuous production for at least six months before the time of investigation."[2] The *ex post* probability of an established entrepreneur indicating that the availability of financial resources was crucial is low. This does not preclude the possibility that, *ex ante*, prospective entrepreneurs (who were not interviewed) were prevented from starting a small industrial unit by a lack of finance. Second, the results are an artifact of the way the research problem was designed. According to Christopher, "the reasons of the respondents for starting a small industry unit were studied in nine categories, namely (1) economic gain, including the desire to earn more money and to give one's children or family a good life; (2) social prestige; (3) social responsibilities, such as giving employment to others; (4) nothing else to do; (5) father's ambition; (6) wife's ambition; (7) own ambition; (8) availability of adequate financial sources; and (9) desire for independence. All these nine reasons were rank ordered for all the sixty-one respondents taken together.[3] However, it is too much to expect a respondent in an interview to rank accurately and meaningfully the strengths of a series of reasons, which are neither comprehensive nor mutually exclusive. But even if the information supplied by the entrepreneur was valid, one should interpret the entrepreneurs as merely indicating that the "availability of adequate financial sources" *is not sufficient,* though perhaps necessary, for starting a small industrial unit.

NOTES

CHAPTER 1

1. Three exceptions are William R. Cline, *Potential Effects of Income Redistribution on Economic Growth: Latin American Cases* (New York: Praeger Publishers, 1972); Irma Adelman and Cynthia Taft Morris, *Economic Growth and Social Equity in Developing Countries* (Stanford: Stanford University Press, 1973); and H. B. Chenery, M. Ahluwalia, C. L. G. Bell, J. Duloy, and R. Jolly, eds., *Redistribution with Growth* (London: Oxford University Press, 1974).

2. Paul A. Baran, *The Political Economy of Growth* (New York: Monthly Review Press, 1957), pp. 254–257.

3. Arthur H. Cole, "An Approach to the Study of Entrepreneurship: A Tribute to Edwin F. Gay," in *Exploration in Enterprise,* ed., Hugh G. J. Aitken (Cambridge: Harvard University Press, 1965), p. 37.

4. Joseph A. Schumpeter, *The Theory of Economic Development: An Inquiry into Profits, Capital, Credit, Interest, and the Business Cycle,* trans., Redvers Opie (New York: Oxford University Press, 1961), pp. 78–79, 93–94 (originally published in 1934).

5. Henry Bernstein, "Modernization Theory and the Sociological Study of Development," *Journal of Development Studies* 7, no. 2 (January 1971): 148.

6. David C. McClelland, *The Achieving Society* (Princeton: D. Van Nostrand Company, 1961), pp. 36–239.

7. Gustav F. Papanek, *Pakistan's Development: Social Goals and Private Incentives* (Cambridge: Harvard University Press, 1967), pp. 2, 25–36, 199.

8. John J. Carroll, *The Filipino Manufacturing Entrepreneur, Agent and Product of Change* (Ithaca: Cornell University Press, 1965), p. 136.

9. Orvis F. Collins, David G. Moore, and Darab B. Unwalla, *The Enterprising Man* (East Lansing, Mich.: MSU Business Studies, 1964), p. 238.

10. John R. Harris, "Nigerian Entrepreneurship in Industry," in *Entrepreneurship and Economic Development,* ed. Peter Kilby (New York: Free Press, 1971), pp. 336–337, and Alec P. Alexander, *Greek Industrialists* (Athens: Center of Planning and Economic Development, 1964), pp. 80–95.

11. Cf. Benjamin Higgins, *Economic Development: Problems, Principles, and Policies* (New York: W. W. Norton, 1968), p. 227.

12. The universe consisted of the entrepreneurs of the fifty-eight private manufacturing establishments that met the following criteria. They had to have been established during the period from 1958 to 1970; had to be at least 50 percent indigenously owned; registered with the Industries Department of Visakhapatnam District; listed as having five or more employees; and operating in the Visakhapatnam municipal area at the time of the interview (January–April 1971). Data were obtained on a sample of fifty-four entrepreneurs, since one entrepreneur headed three firms and another two firms, while in one firm, no appropriate representative could be found for the interview. For the purpose of the analysis, the entrepreneurs with more than one sample firm were identified with the unit they established first. (See Appendix A for an elaboration of methods, procedures, and definitions.)

13. Edward F. Denison, *The Sources of Economic Growth in the United States and the Alternatives before Us* (Supplementary Paper No. 13, Committee for Economic Development, New York, 1962); Robert Solow, "Technical Change and the Aggregate Production Function," *Review of Economics and Statistics* 39, no. 3 (August 1957):312–320; Moses Abramovitz, "Resources and Output Trends in the United States Since 1870," *American Economic Association Papers and Proceedings* 44, no. 2 (May 1956):5–23; and Benton F. Massell, "Capital Formation and Technological Change in United States Manufacturing," *Review of Economics and Statistics* 42, no. 2 (May 1960):182–188.

14. Kanisetti Venkata Ramana, "Caste and Society in an Andhra Town," (Ph.D. diss., University of Illinois, 1971), pp. 21–40.

15. Owens compares the caste composition of his sample in Howrah, West Bengal, to 1931 census data on the distribution of the population by caste. Raymond Owens, "Peasant Entrepreneurs in an Industrial City," in *Entrepreneurship and Modernization of Occupational Cultures in South Asia,* ed. Milton Singer (Durham: Duke University Press, 1973), pp. 136–139. A reliance on information from 1931 is especially inappropriate when considering a rapidly growing industrial city, such as Howrah.

16. Campbell, R. McConnell, *Economics: Principles, Problems, and Policies* (New York: McGraw-Hill, 1972), pp. 530–531.

17. E. Wayne Nafziger, *African Capitalism: A Case Study in Nigerian Entrepreneurship* (Stanford: Hoover Institution, 1977); "The Effect of the Nigerian Extended Family on Entrepreneurial Activity," *Economic Development and Cultural Change* 18, no. 1, pt. 1 (October 1969):25-33; "The Relationship between Education and Entrepreneurship in Nigeria," *The Journal of Developing Areas* 4 (April 1970):349-360; "Interregional Economic Relations in the Nigerian Footwear Industry," *The Journal of Modern African Studies* 6, no. 4 (December 1968):531-542; "A Reconsideration of 'Capital Surplus' in Nigeria," *The Nigerian Journal of Economic and Social Studies*, no. 1 (March 1968): 111-116; and "The Market for Nigerian Entrepreneurs" in *South of the Sahara: Development in African Economies,* ed. Sayre P. Schatz (London: Macmillan, 1972), pp. 61-78.

18. Cf. Yusif A. Sayigh, *Entrepreneurs of Lebanon: The Role of the Business Leader in a Developing Economy* (Cambridge: Harvard University Press, 1962), p. 106.

19. Even the most superficial foreign traveller in India senses that the Western stereotype of the Indian worker, farmer, or businessman as "spiritual" refers to his world-view, which is frequently nonscientific, but not to any lack of a motive for economic gain. In fact, I suspect that the extra satisfaction from the consumption associated with one rupee is greater for the Indian who is living at close to subsistence than for the Westerner living on a much higher income.

20. Sayigh, *Entrepreneurs of Lebanon,* p. 76. His italics.

21. Ibid., pp. 51-120.

22. Central Statistical Organization of India, *Monthly Abstract of Statistics* 28, no. 1 (January 1975):1, and International Bank for Reconstruction and Development, *Trends in Developing Countries* (Washington, 1973), table 14.

23. Everett E. Hagen, *The Economics of Development,* (Homewood, Ill.: Richard D. Irwin, 1968), pp. 7-15; Surendra J. Patel, "The Economic Distance between Nations: Its Origins, Measurement and Outlook," *Economic Journal* 74 (March 1964):122-129; Simon Kuznets, "Levels and Variability of Growth Rates," *Economic Development and Cultural Change* 5, no. 1 (October 1956), pp. 4-9.

24. India, Superintendent of Census Operations, *Census of India 1971, Series 1, India, Paper 1 of 1971—Supplement, Provisional Population Totals* (New Delhi, 1971), p. 62.

25. Statistical Office, Department of Economic and Social Affairs, United Nations, *Statistical Yearbook 1972* (New York, 1973), pp. 602-611.

26. *Census 1971—Supplement, Provisional Population Tables,* p. 51; National Council of Applied Economic Research (N.C.A.E.R.), *Traffic Survey of Visakhapatnam Port* (New Delhi, 1970), p. 1.

27. Visakhapatnam Town Planning Trust, "Draft Report: Visakhama-

hanagar Comprehensive Development Plan, 1969-1986,'' mimeographed, 1968, pp. 3–4.

28. India, Superintendent of Census Operations, *Census of India 1961, Series 2, Andhra Pradesh, Part X-C, District Census Handbook, Visakhapatnam District* (Hyderabad, 1967), p. A.9; Ramana, "Caste and Society," pp. 42–43.

29. K. Sundaram, *Studies in Economic and Social Conditions of Medieval Andhra (A.D. 1000-1600)* (Machilipatnam: Triveni Publishers, 1968).

30. Ramana, "Caste and Society," pp. 48–49; *Census 1961, Handbook, Vizag District,* p. A.17.

31. Ibid, p. A.28; T. Vedantam, *Census of India 1971, Series 2, Andhra Pradesh, Part II-A, General Population Tables* (Hyderabad, 1972), pp. 224–228.

32. N.C.A.E.R., *Traffic Survey,* p. 16; Ramana, "Caste and Society," p. 53.

33. Vendantam, *Census 1971,* pp. 224–228.

CHAPTER 2

1. The important contributions of Max Weber, Everett E. Hagen, Bert F. Hoselitz, and David C. McClelland, which however do not belong in a discussion of the entrepreneur in the history of economic analysis, are discussed in E. Wayne Nafziger, "The Mennonite Ethic in the Weberian Framework," *Explorations in Entrepreneurial History/Second Series* 2, no. 1 (Spring-Summer 1965): 187–204; John R. Harris, "Industrial Entrepreneurship in Nigeria," (Ph.D. diss., Northwestern University, 1967), pp. 40–53; Peter Kilby, ed., *Entrepreneurship and Economic Development* (New York: Free Press, 1971), pp. 1–40. See chapter 3 for a critique of certain aspects of McClelland's views.

2. Richard Cantillon, *Essai sur la Nature Commerce en General* (ca. 1730), ed. and trans. Henry Higgs (London: Frank Cass and Co., 1959), pp. 47–59, 217, 388–399.

3. J. B. Say, *A Treatise on Political Economy,* 4th ed., trans. C. R. Prinsap (Boston: Wells and Lilly, 1824), vol. 2, pp. 55–59.

4. Adam Smith, *An Enquiry into the Nature and Causes of the Wealth of Nations* (London: G. Bell and Sons, 1912), vol. 1, pp. 103, 114–117, 262–264.

5. Say, *Political Economy,* vol. 2, pp. 54–55; and Meenakshi Tyagarajan, "The Development of the Theory of Entrepreneurship," *Indian Economic Review* 4, no. 4 (August 1959):135–150.

6. Alfred Marshall, *Principles of Economies,* 1st ed. (London: Macmillan, 1890), pp. 142, 355, 621, 632–637.

7. Leon Walras, *Elements of Pure Economics or the Theory of Social Wealth* (London: George Allen and Unwin, 1954), pp. 222–223, 225.

8. Stephen Enke, *Economics for Development* (Englewood Cliffs, N.J.: Prentice-Hall, 1963), p. 91.

9. Joseph A. Schumpeter, *Business Cycles*, vol. 1 (New York: McGraw-Hill, 1939), p. 102; *The Theory of Economic Development*, trans. Redvers Opie (New York: Oxford University Press, 1961), pp. 66, 132 (written originally in 1911).

10. Schumpeter, *Business Cycles*, vol. 1, pp. 35–45, 130–132, 235–238.

11. Richard V. Clemence and Francis S. Doody, *The Schumpeterian System* (Cambridge, Mass.: Addison-Wesley Press, 1950), p. 9; Schumpeter, *Business Cycles*, vol. 1, pp. 87–88, 98–102.

12. Schumpeter, *Business Cycles*, vol. 1, pp. 102–104.

13. Ibid., pp. 100–105.

14. Ibid., pp. 87–88, 98–102, 110–111, 123–124, 130–131, 134–137, 158–159; Clemence and Doody, *Schumpeterian System*, pp. 9–10.

15. Schumpeter, *Business Cycles*, vol. 1, p. 145.

16. Hugh G. J. Aitken, "Entrepreneurial Research," in *Explorations in Enterprise*, ed. Hugh Aitken (Cambridge: Harvard University Press, 1965), pp. 8–11, explains why scholars at the Research Center in Entrepreneurial History at Harvard University rejected the Schumpeterian system.

17. Arthur H. Cole, *Business Enterprise in Its Social Setting* (Cambridge: Harvard University Press, 1959), p. 44.

18. W. Robert Maclaurin, "The Sequence from Invention to Innovation and Its Relation to Economic Growth," *Quarterly Journal of Economics* (February 1953):97–111.

19. Frank Knight, *Risk, Uncertainty and Profit* (Boston: Houghton Mifflin Co., 1921), pp. 231–232, 271.

20. Ibid., pp. 141–173, 197.

21. Ibid., pp. 232, 268–270.

22. Ibid., pp. 296–300.

23. Maurice Dobb, *Capitalist Enterprise and Social Progress* (London: Routledge, 1926), pp. 4, 26–41.

24. Ibid., pp. 97–112, 163–164, 172.

25. Ibid., pp. 395–400.

26. William J. Baumol, "Entrepreneurship in Economic Theory," *American Economic Review* 58, no. 2 (May 1968):66–68; Evsey D. Domar, "The Entrepreneur: Discussion," *American Economic Review* 58, no. 2 (May 1968):93.

27. Harvey Leibenstein, "Entrepreneurship and Development," *American Economic Review* 58, no. 2 (May 1968):72.

28. Leibenstein, ibid., pp. 72–77, and "Allocative Efficiency vs. 'X-Efficiency,'" *American Economic Review* 56, no. 3 (June 1966):392–415.

29. Leibenstein refers to works such as those I have cited in note 13 in chapter 1.

30. Leibenstein, "Entrepreneurship," pp. 77–83.

31. James H. Soltow, "The Entrepreneur in Economic History," *American Economic Review* 58, no. 2 (May 1968):84–92.

32. Alfred Marshall, who suggests that "[t]he task of directing production . . . is so difficult . . . that it has to be broken up and given into the hands of a specialized body of employers, . . . or business men" (pp. 354–355), does not make use of the idea any further in his treatise. See Alfred Marshall, *Principles of Economics* (London: Macmillan, 1890), pp. 365, 371.

33. Frederick Harbison, "Entrepreneurial Organization as a Factor in Economic Development," *Quarterly Journal of Economics* 64, no. 3 (August 1956):365–367. Cf. Cole, *Business Enterprise,* p. 44.

34. Pritam Singh, "Essays Concerning Some Types of Entrepreneurship in India," (Ph.D. diss., University of Michigan, 1963), pp. 8–10.

35. Schumpeter, *Business Cycles,* vol. 1, p. 102, and "Economic Theory and Entrepreneurial History," in *Change and the Entrepreneur,* Harvard University Research Center in Entrepreneurial History (Cambridge: Harvard University Press, 1949), p. 68.

36. Cf., however, Douglas Rimmer, "Schumpeter and the Underdeveloped Countries," *Quarterly Journal of Economics* 75, no. 3 (August 1961): 433–450.

37. Schumpeter did not consider the imitator to be an entrepreneur. Nevertheless, see Henry G. Aubrey, "Industrial Investment Decisions," *Journal of Economic History* 15 (December 1955):338; Margaret Katzin, "The Role of the Small Entrepreneur," in *Economic Transition in Africa,* eds. Melville J. Herskovits and Mitchel Harwitz (Evanston: Northwestern University Press, 1964), p. 183; James J. Berna, *Industrial Entrepreneurship in Madras State* (New York: Asia Publishing House, 1960), p. 4. Joseph A. Schumpeter, in *The Theory of Economic Development,* pp. 132, 229–230 and *Business Cycles,* vol. 1, pp. 102, 131, 137 has contrasted the "imitating" entrepreneur with the "innovating" entrepreneur. Entrepreneurs who adapt innovations already in existence could be said to be involved in both imitation and innovation.

38. On the other hand, even Schumpeter's "new combinations" involve a degree of imitation. The history of technological change provides few abrupt breaks from the past. T. S. Ashton, *The Industrial Revolution* (New York: Oxford University Press, 1948), p. 2.

39. Sayigh (see text discussion in this chapter) is probably more successful than any other researcher in translating the modified Schumpeterian concept into a working definition. Nevertheless, it is unlikely that another investigator working independently would agree with Sayigh in his selection of 207 innovators.

40. The crucial decision in the firm is the selection of men to make deci-

sions. "Any other sort of decision making or exercise of judgment is automatically reduced to a routine function" (Knight, *Risk, Uncertainty and Profit,* pp. 296–298).

41. Even though there are a large number of family enterprises in Visakhapatnam, one can readily distinguish the principal of the firm, who is usually the father or eldest brother. Typically, after the death or retirement of the father, his eldest surviving brother or eldest son eventually becomes the principal in the family's business empire, although this is not automatic where the eldest lacks interest or a younger brother or cousin is definitely more competent.

42. Nor, in principle, would all Schumpeterian entrepreneurs in sample firms be included in the list of fifty-four entrepreneurs I have analyzed. In fact, however, the firms tended to be so dominated by one man that no Schumpeterian entrepreneur was found outside this list. (See chapter 4 and Appendix B.)

43. John R. Harris, "Industrial Entrepreneurship in Nigeria," (Ph.D. diss., Northwestern University, August 1967), pp. 40–71.

44. Peter Kilby, ed., *Entrepreneurship and Economic Development* (New York: The Free Press, 1971), pp. 1–40.

45. Yusif A. Sayigh, *Entrepreneurs of Lebanon: The Role of Business Leader in a Developing Economy* (Cambridge: Harvard University Press, 1962).

46. John J. Carroll, *The Filipino Manufacturing Entrepreneur: Agent and Product of Change* (Ithaca: Cornell University Press, 1965).

47. Alec P. Alexander, *Greek Industrialists: An Economic and Social Analysis* (Athens: Center of Planning and Economic Research, 1964).

48. Gustav F. Papanek, "The Development of Entrepreneurship," *American Economic Review* 52 (May 1962):48–58, and *Pakistan's Development: Social Goals and Private Incentives* (Cambridge: Harvard University Press, 1967).

49. E. Wayne Nafziger, *African Capitalism;* "Nigerian Extended Family," pp. 25–33; "Education and Entrepreneurship," pp. 349–360; "Nigerian Footwear Industry," pp. 531–542; "Reconsideration," pp. 111–116; and "Nigerian Entrepreneurs," pp. 61–78.

50. John R. Harris, "Industrial Entrepreneurship"; and "Nigerian Entrepreneurship in Industry," in Kilby, ed. *Entrepreneurship and Economic Development,* pp. 331–355.

51. Berna, *Industrial Entrepreneurship.*

52. Sayigh, *Entrepreneurs of Lebanon,* pp. 12–50.

53. Ibid., pp. 69–79.

54. Carroll, *Filipino Manufacturing Entrepreneur,* pp. 97–98.

55. A. P. Alexander, *Greek Industrialists,* p. 15.

56. Alec P. Alexander, "Industrial Entrepreneurship in Turkey: Origins and Growth," *Economic Development and Cultural Change* 8, no. 4, pt. 1 (July 1960):350–355.

57. Papanek, "Entrepreneurship," pp. 46–58.

58. Everett E. Hagen, "Discussion," *American Economic Review* 52: 59–61. I mention the Hagen-Papanek controversy as a parallel to the Hoselitz-Berna debate, discussed in chapter 3.

59. Nafziger, "Nigerian Entrepreneurs," pp. 61–78.

60. Nafziger, "Education and Entrepreneurship," pp. 349–360.

61. Nafziger, "Effect of Nigerian Extended Family," pp. 25–33.

62. Nafziger, "Nigerian Footwear Industry," pp. 521–542.

63. Harris, "Nigerian Entrepreneurship," p. 337.

64. Robert A. LeVine, *Dreams and Deeds: Achievement Motivation in Nigeria* (Chicago: University of Chicago Press, 1966).

65. Carroll, "Filipino Manufacturing Entrepreneur," p. 100.

66. In my study of Nigerian entrepreneurs, I used rate of profit and the value of output as indices of business success.

67. Harris, "Nigerian Entrepreneurship," pp. 340–342.

CHAPTER 3

1. Ruddat Datt and K. P. M. Sundharam, *Indian Economy* (New Delhi: Niraj Prakashan, 1968), p. 144.

2. Dhananjaya Ramchandra Gadgil, *Origins of the Modern Indian Business Class—An Interim Report* (New York: Institute of Pacific Relations, 1959).

3. Phiroze B. Medhora, "Entrepreneurship in India," *Political Science Quarterly* 80, no. 4 (September 1965):558–559.

4. Datt and Sundharam, *Indian Economy,* pp. 144–146.

5. Radhe Shyam Rungta, *The Rise of Business Corporations in India 1851–1900* (Cambridge: Cambridge University Press, 1970), p. 19.

6. Helen B. Lamb, "The Rise of Indian Business Communities," *Pacific Affairs* 23, no. 2 (June 1955):105.

7. R. Balakrishna, *Review of Economic Growth in India* (Bangalore: Bangalore Press, 1961), p. 102.

8. Gunnar K. Myrdal, *Asian Drama—An Inquiry into the Poverty of Nations,* vol. 1 (Middlesex: Penguin, 1968):710–712.

9. Datt and Sundharam, *Indian Economy,* p. 50; Pritam Singh, "Essays Concerning Some Types of Entrepreneurship in India," (Ph.D. diss., University of Michigan, 1963), pp. 38–40.

10. Jagdish N. Bhagwati and Padma Desai, *India: Planning for Industrialization: Industrialization and Trade Policies since 1951* (London: Oxford University Press, 1970), p. 267.

11. Harold A. Gould, "The Adaptive Functions of Caste in Contemporary Indian Society," *Asian Survey* 3, no. 9 (September 1963):427–428; M. N. Srinivas, *Caste in Modern India and Other Essays* (New York: Asia Publishing House, 1962), pp. 63, 69; Lloyd I. Rudolph and Susanne Hoeber Rudolph, *The Modernity of Tradition: Political Development in India* (Chicago: University of Chicago Press, 1967), p. 119.

12. Srinivas, *Caste,* pp. 7–8, 42, 65.

13. The Jains, an ascetic religious sect originating in the ancient period, became a trading sect for purely ritualistic reasons—only in trading could one practice ahimsa (the absolute prohibition of the killing of living things). [Max Weber, *The Religion of India—The Sociology of Hinduism and Buddhism* (New York: The Free Press, 1958), pp. 199–204.] The transition from trading to manufacturing by Jains (especially Marwari Jains) in the second or third decade of the twentieth century was a definite break with scriptural teachings. Medhora suggests that this may have been possible because of the strong influence of the Jain laity. [Medhora, "Entrepreneurship in India," pp. 565–566.]

14. Gadgil, *Modern Indian Business Class,* pp. 16–21.

15. Amalendu Guha, "Parsi Seths as Entrepreneurs, 1750–1850," *Economic and Political Weekly* 5 (29 August 1970):M.107–M.115; and "The Comprador Role of Parsi Seths, 1750–1850," *Economic and Political Weekly* 5 (28 November 1970):1933–1936.

16. The Parsis, followers of Zoroaster who migrated from Iran to western India 1300 years ago, have no basic roots within the country. Medhora, "Entrepreneurship in India," p. 564.

17. Lamb, "Indian Business Communities," pp. 104–105.

18. Howard Spodek, "The Manchesterisation of Ahmedabad," *Economic Weekly* 17 (13 March 1965):483–490; and "Traditional Culture and Entrepreneurship: A Case Study of Ahmedabad," *Economic and Political Weekly* 4 (22 February 1969), pp. M.27–M.31; Spodek and Kenneth L. Gillion, *Ahmedabad: A Study in Indian Urban History* (Berkeley: University of California Press, 1968), pp. 74–104, relate the story of Ranchhodlal Chhotalal, a local Nagar Brahmin dismissed from the civil service for allegedly accepting a bribe and an outsider among the Bania trading community, who was instrumental in starting production in the first successful textile mill in Ahmedabad in 1861.

19. Blair B. Kling, "Obstacles to Entrepreneurship in India: The Case of Bengal" (Paper presented to the Congress of Orientalists, University of Michigan, Ann Arbor, August 1967), pp. 1–17.

20. Ibid.

21. Ibid., pp. 4–5, 12; Lamb, "Indian Business Communities," pp. 105–109; and Thomas A. Timberg, *Industrial Entrepreneurship among the*

Trading Communities of India: How the Pattern Differs, Center for International Affairs, Development Advisory Service, Economic Development Report no. 136, Harvard University, July 1969, pp. 21–48.

22. Timberg, *Trading Communities,* pp. 21–48, and Lamb, "Indian Business Communities," pp. 98–126. Timberg investigates why the Marwaris and Gujarati Hindu trading communities are disproportionately represented among large industrial entrepreneurs, and why Bengalis and Gujarati Muslim trading communities have little representation. The sample, researched on the basis of written documents and publications, comprises the thirty-seven largest North-Indian-owned industrial houses as listed in the Monopolies Inquiry Commission Report of 1964. He explains business activity in terms of the structure of economic opportunites and the evolution of historical events, rather than in terms of motivation, ideology, and character traits, which are in part derived from the nature of the economic and political systems.

23. Leighton W. Hazlehurst, *Entrepreneurship and the Merchant Castes in a Punjabi City* (Durham: Duke University Commonwealth Studies Center, 1966), pp. 1–5. In 1966, when the state of Punjab was divided into two states, the city became a part of northeastern Haryana.

24. Ibid., pp. 15–19, 119–120.

25. Ibid., pp. 28–33, 40–45.

26. Ibid., pp. 45–54.

27. Ibid., pp. 55–59, 118–119.

28. Owens, "Peasant Entrepreneurs," pp. 133–166.

29. Nafziger, "Education and Entrepreneurs," pp. 355–357.

30. Berna, *Industrial Entrepreneurship,* pp. 1–4, 224.

31. Ibid., pp. 42–44, 83–86.

32. Ibid., pp. 212–213.

33. Bert F. Hoselitz, "Entrepreneurship and Traditional Elites," *Explorations in Entrepreneurial History/Second Series* 1, no. 1 (Fall 1963):36–39.

34. Nafziger, *African Capitalism,* pp. 126–148.

35. Papanek, "Entrepreneurship," pp. 46–58; Everett E. Hagen, "Problems of Economic Development—Discussion," *American Economic Review* 52, no. 2 (May 1962):59–61.

36. Berna, *Industrial Entrepreneurship,* pp. 60–70.

37. Max Weber, *The Religion of India—The Sociology of Hinduism and Buddhism* (New York: The Free Press, 1958).

38. Max Weber, *The Protestant Ethic and the Spirit of Capitalism,* trans. Talcott Parsons (New York: Charles Scribner's Sons, 1958).

39. E. Wayne Nafziger, "The Mennonite Ethic in the Weberian Framework," *Explorations in Entrepreneurial History/Second Series 2,* no. 1 (Spring/Summer 1965):187–204; R. H. Tawney, *Religion and the Rise of Capitalism* (New York: Harcourt Brace and Co., 1926); and Kurt

Samuelsson, *Religion and Economic Action: A Critique of Max Weber* (New York: Harper and Row, 1964).

40. Milton Singer, *When a Great Tradition Modernizes* (New York: Praeger Publications, 1972), pp. 272–280. See Nafziger, "Mennonite Ethic," pp. 187–204, for a discussion of worldly asceticism, concept of the "calling," and the explanation of prosperity by Weber's Puritan capitalist.

41. Gadgil, *Modern Indian Business Class*, p. 16; Weber, *Religion of India*, p. 24; and Medhora, "Entrepreneurship in India," pp. 558–580.

42. Bert F. Hoselitz, *Sociological Aspects of Economic Growth* (New York: The Free Press, 1960), p. 155.

43. Irawati Karve, *Hindu Society—An Interpretation* (Poona: Sangam Press Private Ltd., 1961), pp. 94–95; and Weber, *Religion of India*, pp. 24–25.

44. George B. Baldwin, *Industrial Growth in South India—Case Studies in Economic Development* (New York: The Free Press, 1959), p. 338.

45. McKim Marriott, *Caste Ranking and Community Structure in Five Regions of India and Pakistan* (Poona: Deccan College Postgraduate and Research Institute, 1965), pp. 21–25.

46. Ibid.; and Marriott, "Caste Ranking and Food Transactions: A Matrix Analysis," in *Structure and Change in Indian Society*, eds. Milton Singer and Bernard S. Cohn (Chicago: Aldine Publishing Co., 1968), pp. 164–166.

47. Srinivas, *Caste*, pp. 193–194.

48. Marriott, "Caste Ranking," p. 166.

49. Ibid., p. 168; Medhora, "Entrepreneurship in India," p. 564.

50. M. N. Srinivas, "Mobility in the Caste System," in *Structure and Change in Indian Society*, eds., Milton Singer and Bernard S. Cohn (Chicago: Aldine Publishing Co., 1968), p. 197.

51. Hazlehurst, *Entrepreneurship and Merchant Castes*, pp. 26–54; and Weber, *The Protestant Ethic*, p. 191.

52. Hazlehurst, *Entrepreneurship and Merchant Castes*, pp. 35–40.

53. Srinivas, "Mobility in the Caste System," p. 194.

54. Medhora, "Entrepreneurship in India," p. 564.

55. Hazlehurst, "Caste and Merchant Communities," in *Structure and Change in Indian Society*, eds. Milton Singer and Bernard Cohn (Chicago: Aldine Publishing Co., 1968), p. 295.

56. Hazlehurst, *Entrepreneurship and Merchant Castes*, pp. 26–54.

57. Srinivas, "Mobility in the Caste System," pp. 194–196; and Hazlehurst, *Entrepreneurship and Merchant Castes*, pp. 49–51.

58. Lamb, "Indian Business Communities," p. 102.

59. Spodek, "Manchesterisation of Ahmedabad," p. 488.

60. Nafziger, "Effect of the Nigerian Extended Family," pp. 25–33; see

R. A. Sharma, "Emerging Patterns of Industrial Entrepreneurship in India," *Developing Economies* 11, no. 1 (March 1973): 41, for a dissenting view.

61. Hazlehurst, *Entrepreneurship and Merchant Castes*, pp. 42–45, 97.

62. Ibid., pp. 45, 109–118.

63. Ibid., pp. 47–48. Compare Robert A. LeVine's discussion of the patron-client relationship among the Hausa in northern Nigeria in *Dreams and Deeds: Achievement Motivation in Nigeria* (Chicago: The University of Chicago Press, 1966), pp. 25–32.

64. Cf. Rungta, *Business Corporations*, pp. 223–231; Andrew F. Brimmer, "The Setting of Entrepreneurship in India," *Quarterly Journal of Economics* 29, no. 4 (November 1955): 559–560; Blair B. Kling, "The Origins of the Managing Agency System in India," *Journal of Asian Studies* 26, no. 1 (November 1966): 37–38; and Singh, "Types of Entrepreneurship," pp. 58–59 on the origins of the system. A determination of the extent to which the managing agency was an Indian contribution, as Kling argues, or of British origin, as Rungta maintains in *Business Corporations* (pp. 235–255) must wait for further research.

65. Singh, "Types of Entrepreneurship," p. 57.

66. Brimmer, "Setting of Entrepreneurship," p. 554.

67. Singh, "Types of Entrepreneurship," pp. 59–61.

68. Brimmer, "Setting of Entrepreneurship," pp. 554–555.

69. Timberg, *Trading Communities*, p. 11.

70. Ibid., p. 558.

71. Singh, "Types of Entrepreneurship," pp. 59–61.

72. Ibid., pp. 61–62.

73. Brimmer, "Setting of Entrepreneurship," pp. 560–561.

74. See Singh, "Types of Entrepreneurship," pp. 59–61.

75. Ibid., pp. 71–73.

76. Joseph A. Schumpeter, *Capitalism, Socialism and Democracy* (New York: Harper and Row, 1942), pp. 87–106.

77. Singh, "Types of Entrepreneurship," p. 73.

78. David C. McClelland and David G. Winter, *Motivating Economic Achievement—Accelerating Economic Development through Psychological Training* (New York: The Free Press, 1971).

79. Everett E. Hagen, *The Economics of Development* (Homewood, Ill.: Richard D. Irwin, 1975), pp. 282–283; and McClelland and Winter, *Motivating Economic Achievement*, pp. 39–41.

80. David C. McClelland, *The Achieving Society*, (Princeton: D. Van Nostrand Company, 1961). I make no attempt to undertake a comprehensive evaluation, as the work has been widely reviewed and criticized. Economists who have reviewed the McClelland theses include Sayre P. Schatz, "n Achievement and Economic Growth: A Critical Appraisal," *Quarterly Jour-*

nal of Economics 79, no. 2 (May 1965): 234–241; Benjamin Higgins, *Economic Development Problems, Principles, and Policies* (New York: W. W. Norton, 1968), pp. 241–249; Peter Kilby, ed., *Entrepreneurship and Economic Development* (New York: The Free Press, 1971), pp. 7–11, 15–21; and Fritz Redlich, "Economic Development, Entrepreneurship, and Psychologism," *Explorations in Entrepreneurial History/Second Series* 1, no. 1 (Fall 1963): 10–35.

81. McClelland and Winter, *Motivating Economic Achievement*, p. 2.

82. This is despite the authors' cognizance of Eisenstadt's criticism that research on n Ach neglects social-structural variables. Ibid., pp. 15, 312.

83. Ibid., p. 362.

84. Ibid., pp. 39–175.

85. Jai B. P. Sinha, "The n-Ach/n-Cooperation under Limited/Unlimited Resource Conditions," *Journal of Experimental Social Psychology* 4 (1968): 233–246.

86. McClelland and Winter, *Motivating Economic Achievement*, pp. 123–125, 250–251.

87. Ibid., pp. 60, 71–72, 150.

88. Gloria V. Javillonar and George R. Peters, "Sociological and Social Psychological Aspects of Indian Entrepreneurship," *British Journal of Sociology* 24, no. 3 (September 1973): 314–328.

89. McClelland and Winter, *Motivating Economic Achievement*, pp. 26, 154–155, 159, 337.

90. Ashis Nandy, Review of *Motivating Economic Achievement* in *Economic Development and Cultural Change*, 20, no. 3 (April 1972): 578.

91. McClelland and Winter, *Motivating Economic Achievement*, pp. 66, 117–137.

92. Ibid., pp. 126–128, 313–319.

93. It is possible that this could not have been done without misunderstanding, harmful to the overall program.

94. The participants "first take a form of the Thematic Apperception Test in which they write imaginative stories about a series of pictures. They then learn how to code what they have written according to the standard system for identifying *n* Achievement . . . . They then rewrite the stories at various times, trying to maximize the number of scoring categories they can introduce . . . . Few can [obtain a maximum score] without considerable practice, but most are able after a few lessons to get much higher scores than they did at first.

"The idea behind this training is very simple. It is to form the associative network, which in a certain sense could be considered the motive itself." McClelland and Winter, *Motivating Economic Achievement*, pp. 46–47.

95. Ibid., pp. 324–328.

96. Ibid., pp. 258, 268, 271–272.

97. Nandy, "Review," p. 578.

98. Kilby, *Entrepreneurship and Economic Development*, p. 21.

99. A. D. Pabaney, Elliot Danzig, M. S. Nadkarni, Udai Pareek, and David C. McClelland, "Developing the Entrepreneurial Spirit in the Indian Community," Small Industries Extension Training Institute and Harvard University, Working Report, Hyderabad, India, September 20, 1964.

100. McClelland and Winter, *Motivating Economic Achievement,* pp. 189, 297.

101. Ibid., pp. 215, 217, 221, 226.

102. Kilby, *Entrepreneurship*, p. 21. Although the Working Report cited in note 99 suggests that the entrepreneurs were to report profits, McClelland and Winter, *Motivating Economic Achievement*, provide no information on these data. The decrease in entrepreneurial efficiency and returns suggests the possibility that profits increased less among course participants than in the "control groups."

103. McClelland, *Achieving Society*, p. 362, based on Bernard C. Rosen, "Race, Ethnicity and the Achievement Syndrome,"*American Sociological Review* 24, no. 1 (February 1959): 51–52.

104. LeVine, *Dreams and Deeds*, pp. 48, 56–57.

105. See Oscar Lewis, *La Vida: A Puerto Rican Family in the Culture of Poverty—San Juan and New York* (New York: Vintage Books, 1968), pp. xlii–lii; and William H. Grier and Price M. Cobbs, *Black Rage* (New York: Bantam Books, 1968).

106. McClelland and Winter, *Motivating Economic Achievement* p. 9.

107. Ironically, the only references to a measure of n Ach among Indian entrepreneurs who were trained are in the context of a comparison of the precourse scores of entrepreneurs who were active and those inactive after the course, and the aggregate trend in n Ach scores of participants from before the training to two to three years later. Ibid., pp. 270, 324–330.

108. Furthermore, in the same year a series of application forms and written tests designed by the Behavioural Science Centre in Delhi were used, together with interviews, to aid administrators in selecting trainees. Analysis of the tests were employed, inter alia, to identify those applicants with a high n Ach.

109. Richard Morse, "Local Entrepreneurial Initiatives and Development in the Philippines, Malaysia, Indonesia and India: Research Observations," East-West Technology and Development Institute, Honolulu, 18 February 1975, unpublished report, pp. 13–14; and Robert B. Buchele, *The Development of Small Industrial Entrepreneurs as a Tool of Economic Growth*, East-West Technology and Development Institute Working Paper no. 31, (Honolulu, October 1972), pp. 28–33. I am indebted to Richard Morse for providing materials on the NIMID, MSSIDC, and the Gujarat Program.

110. Morse, "Local Initiatives," p. 14.

111. Buchele, *Small Entrepreneurs*, p. 29.
112. Ibid., p. 33; Morse, "Local Initiatives," p. 14.
113. Maharashtra Small Scale Industries Development Corporation (MSSIDC), "Entrepreneurship Development Clinic—Instructions for Filling the Application Form," (Bombay: Mouj Printing Bureau, 1974), p. 3.
114. A new entrepreneurial venture may often require a combination of motivation, appropriate management and technical skills, financial resources, and access to input quotas. In several cases, the Gujarat program has assisted the prospective entrepreneur in acquiring capital and licenses, in addition to motivational and management training.
115. Berna, *Industrial Entrepreneurship*, p. 146.

CHAPTER 4

1. Ramana, "Caste and Society," pp. 132-134, 139-140.
2. Statistics of Vizag are based on the universe of 2,000 households from eight representative areas within the city as indicated in Ramana, "Caste and Society," pp. 21-29, a source consistent with the 1961 census data on the distribution of the population of Vizag city by religion. The classification of the *jatis* of in-state entrepreneurs according to *varna* is indicated in Appendix B.
3. The one Christian in the sample is not an exception to this generalization. He belongs to the Syrian Christians from Kerala, considered, because of the early origins of their religion in India (the first to fourth century A.D.), their emphasis on ritual purification, their endogamy, and their reputation as traders and technicians, to approximate closely the caste standing of the Kerala Kshatriya. Aziz S. Atiya, *The History of Eastern Christianity* (London: Methuen and Co., 1968), p. 377.
4. Ramana, "Caste and Society," pp. 130-131.
5. Calculated value of $\chi^2 = 9.70$, $\chi^2_{.01}$ with 1 d.f. = 6.64.
6. The *average* initial equity capital is Rs. 191,000 for twice-born castes compared to Rs. 64,000 for Sudras. Calculated value of $\chi^2 = 59,753.52$, $\chi^2_{.01}$ with 1 d.f. = 6.64.
7. The percentage of entrepreneurs from twice-born castes with a bachelor's degree is significantly higher than the percentage of Sudras. Calculated value of $\chi^2 = 6.49$, $\chi^2_{.02}$ with 1 d.f. = 5.41.
8. The percentage of businessmen from high castes with prior managerial responsibility was significantly higher than the percentage of Sudras. Calculated value of $\chi^2 = 5.76$, $\chi^2_{.02}$ with 1 d.f. = 5.41.
9. Ramana, "Caste and Society," pp. 131-141, 198, 200.
10. Cf. T. S. Epstein, *Economic Development and Social Change in South Asia* (Manchester: University Press, 1962), pp. 243-254, 276-278, 293.
11. A comment by Koppel and Peterson on the Naidu illustrates the danger of separating an analysis of ethnic, caste, and religious communities from their social and historical context. The authors refer to evidence that the Nai-

dus were overrepresented in my sample and most successful in terms of level and growth of employment among Berna's respondents in Tamil Nadu, while at the same time underrepresented among the family entrepreneurs in Sharma's study. This inconsistency, among other things, is a basis for suggesting "that there is no *abiding* and *generalized* relationship between entrepreneurial success and groups of individuals distributed over regions and over time" [their italics]. Bruce Koppel and Richard E. Peterson, "Industrial Entrepreneurship in India: A Reevaluation," *Developing Economies* 13 (September 1975):328–330. (Studies cited are E. Wayne Nafziger, "South Indian Industrialists: A Profile of Entrepreneurs in Coastal Andhra," East-West Technology and Development Institute Working Paper no. 34 [December 1972]; Berna, *Industrial Entrepreneurship;* R. A. Sharma, "Emerging Patterns of Industrial Entrepreneurship in India," *Developing Economies* 11 [March 1973]:39–61.) However, since Naidus are a south Indian community with no pattern of migration to other regions, it is to be expected that Naidus would not be highly represented in Sharma's all-India data, in which the overwhelming majority of firms are located in northern and central India. (My criticisms borrow from an unpublished comment by Richard Morse.) Analogously, data indicating a low representation of Christians in India, where they are primarily from low castes, and a high representation in Lebanon and southern Nigeria, where they have formed a disproportionate share of the economic and political leadership, are not contradictory.

12. For more details, see Thomas A. Timberg, *Industrial Entrepreneurship among the Trading Communities of India: How the Pattern Differs,* Center for International Affairs, Harvard University, 1969, pp. 17–18; Rungta, pp. 165–167; and chapter 3.

13. Cf. Morris D. Morris, "Values as an Obstacle to Economic Growth in South Asia: An Historical Survey," *Journal of Economic History* 27 (December 1967): 604.

14. In order to arrive at the entrepreneur's perception of capacity utilization, I asked the following question: "Assume that the price of your products remains the same, and that you use the same plant and equipment. How much more could you have produced (in rupee value) in 1969/70 if you could have sold all that you produced?" (See Appendix A, question 32.) In four of the eight instances, capacity utilization for one shift was perceived by the entrepreneurs to be less than 50 percent.

15. Kusum Nair, *Blossoms in the Dust: The Human Factor in Indian Development* (New York: Praeger Publishers, 1962), pp. 102–15.

16. N. A. Rao, "The Commercial Entrepreneurs in Visakhapatnam City: A Survey," (Waltair: Department of Cooperation and Applied Economics, Andhra University, 1971), pp. 30–31.

17. The median personal income of the entrepreneurs was low, partly

because of the fact that only one of the entrepreneurs was involved in other businesses.

18. E. Wayne Nafziger, "Indian Entrepreneurship: A Survey," in *Entrepreneurship and Economic Development*, ed. Peter Kilby (New York: Free Press, 1971), pp. 299–300; Hoselitz, "Entrepreneurship and Traditional Elites," pp. 36–40; Berna, *Industrial Entrepreneurship*, pp. 42–44, 83–86, 212–213.

19. Owens, "Peasant Entrepreneurs," p. 147.

20. Ramana, "Caste and Society," pp. 120, 134.

21. Out-of-state entrepreneurs are overrepresented in the sample of entrepreneurs by a highly significant amount (see table 8).

22. For a parallel, see Werner Sombart's discussion of Jewish entrepreneurs in the Middle Ages, *Die Juden und das Wirtschaftsleben* (Munich: Verlag von Duncker and Humbolt, 1928).

23. Government of India, *Economic Survey 1970–71* (Delhi, 1971), p. 78.

24. Calculated value of $\chi^2 = 379.57$, $\chi^2_{.01}$ with 2 d.f. $= 9.21$.

25. Schumpeter, *Business Cycles,* vol. 1, pp. 102–104.

26. Fifty-nine percent of Schumpeterian entrepreneurs received most or all of their initial capital from the family, and 88 percent received at least partial assistance from the family. These figures indicate, perhaps surprisingly, that the Schumpeterian entrepreneurs were at least as dependent upon the family for initial funds as other entrepreneurs. Cf. the discussion in chapter 5.

27. The percentages of Schumpeterian entrepreneurs born outside India (18 percent), within India but outside Andhra Pradesh (35 percent), and within Andhra Pradesh but outside Vizag District (29 percent) exceed those percentages for the fifty-four sample entrepreneurs. This is consistent with, though not firm evidence of, my observation above that immigrants originate from a select portion of the population, and are more likely to be innovative than others (see the discussion on birthplace in this chapter).

28. See Dobb's views, as outlined in chapter 2.

29. John R. Harris, "Nigerian Entrepreneurship in Industry," in *Entrepreneurship and Economic Development*, ed. Peter Kilby (New York: Free Press, 1971), p. 336; Alexander, *Greek Industrialists,* pp. 139–142; and Carroll, *Filipino Manufacturing Entrepreneur,* pp. 90–91.

30. R. K. Hazari, *The Structure of the Corporate Private Sector: A Study of Concentration, Ownership and Control* (Bombay: Asia Publishing House, 1966); Lamb, "Indian Business Communities," pp. 101–116; Medhora, "Entrepreneurship in India," pp. 562–578; Timberg, *Trading Communities of India,* pp. 4–5, 81–82; Gadgil, *Modern Indian Business Class,* p. 59; and others surveyed in chapter 3.

31. Berna, *Industrial Entrepreneurship,* pp. 43, 83.

32. Papanek, "Development of Entrepreneurship," pp. 50–58.

33. S. B. Prasad and A. R. Negandhi, *Managerialism for Economic Development: Essays on India* (The Hague: Martinus Nijhoff, 1968), p. 27. Compare table 10, although it is not strictly comparable.

34. Richard D. Lambert, *Workers, Factories, and Social Change in India* (Princeton: Princeton University Press, 1963), pp. 33-34, 36-38.

CHAPTER 5

1. Although variations in the definitions and scope of economic sectors pose some difficulty in making comparisons, studies of Greek, Filipino, Pakistani, and Nigerian entrepreneurs suggest that with the exception of those previously in manufacturing, former traders and merchants tend to be the most successful industrialists. Alexander, *Greek Industrialists,* pp. 49-51; Carroll, *Filipino Manufacturing Entrepreneur,* pp. 73-74; Papanek, "Development of Entrepreneurship," pp. 45-58; Peter Kilby, *African Enterprise: The Nigerian Bread Industry* (Stanford: Hoover Institution on War, Revolution, and Peace, 1965), pp. 93-94.

2. See James T. McCrory, *Case Studies in Latent Industrial Potential: Small Industry in a North Indian Town* (Delhi: Government of India, Ministry of Commerce and Industry, 1956), pp. 9-16, and Carroll, *Filipino Manufacturing Entrepreneur,* pp. 168-172.

Rungta, *Business Corporations* pp. 56-57 maintains, "Mercantile discipline does not provide the right kind of thrust to break through difficult barriers, inasmuch as merchants tend to lack tenacity of purpose, the *sine qua non* of a true entrepreneur."

3. See chapter 4.

4. Berna, *Industrial Entrepreneurship,* pp. 44-49; Nafziger, *African Capitalism,* pp. 163-165; John R. Harris, "Industrial Entrepreneurship in Nigeria" (Ph.D. Diss., Northwestern University, 1967), pp. 272-299.

5. E. Wayne Nafziger, "The Political Economy of Disintegration in Nigeria," *Journal of Modern African Studies* 11, no. 4 (December 1973):508-522.

6. McCrory, *Latent Industrial Potential,* pp. 3-4.

7. Hazari, *Corporate Private Sector,* p. 344.

8. There is a significant positive relationship between initial share capital (Y) and the number of years of management and entrepreneurial experience prior to the establishment of the business (X). $Y = 35,661.62500 + 12,089.4765$, $t = 2.82741$. The regression coefficient is significant at the 1 percent level.

9. Carroll, *Filipino Manufacturing Entrepreneur,* p. 42; Collins, Moore, and Unwalla, *The Enterprising Man,* pp. 232-233.

10. Cf. Nafziger, "Education and Entrepreneurship," p. 354.

11. Ibid., p. 357; V. N. Kothari, "Disparities in Relative Earnings among Different Countries," *Economic Journal* 80 (September 1970):606.

12. For an explanation of an instance where education is negatively related to entrepreneurial success, see Nafziger, "Education and Entrepreneurship," pp. 355-388.

13. Ramana, "Caste and Society," p. 134.

14. Nafziger, "Effect of Nigerian Extended Family," p. 29.

15. Where Y is initial share capital and X is the number of the entrepreneur's relatives in the firm, Y = 57,508.50000 + 50, 433.53125X, t = 2.609, and the regression coefficient is significant at the 2 percent level.

16. Entrepreneurs with a high paternal economic status had an *average* initial capital of Rs. 319,000 compared to Rs. 66,000 for those with a medium or low economic status. Calculated value of $\chi^2 = 302,053.43$, $\chi^2_{.01}$ with 1 d.f. = 6.64.

17. By and large, partners in the firm did not receive financial support from relatives outside the firm for expansion purposes, as relatives expect growth to be funded by retained earnings. In fact, as the firm expands the number of dependents the entrepreneur is required to support also increases. If Y is the number of dependents of the major entrepreneur and X the percentage growth of the production of the firm in the five years prior to fiscal year, 1969/70, Y = −0.21450 + 0.12522X, t = 2.29183, and the regression coefficient is significant at the 5 percent level. Cf. Nafziger, "Effect of Nigerian Extended Family," pp. 30-32.

CHAPTER 6

1. William Bredo, *Industrial Estates* (Glencoe: The Free Press, 1960), pp. 1-2.

2. P. C. Alexander, *Industrial Estates in India* (Bombay: Asia Publishing House, 1963), pp. 5-6.

3. Wolfgang F. Stolper, *Planning without Facts: Lessons in Resource Allocation from Nigeria's Development* (Cambridge: Harvard University Press, 1966), pp. 166, 280; Sayre P. Schatz, "African Capitalism: Development Policy in Nigeria," chapter 6; Tibor Scitovsky, "Two Concepts of External Economies," *Journal of Political Economy* 62 (April 1954): 143-151.

4. Alexander, *Industrial Estates,* pp. 57-60.

5. Experience indicates that large industrial houses prefer to train their own personnel, and do not utilize extension training and consulting services, even when available. Nevertheless, those who do utilize the service, the less prosperous entrepreneurs, are still likely to have incomes higher than the average in India. My own view is, however, that the positive spillovers mentioned above outweigh the slightly negative effect on income distribution.

6. Jagdish N. Bhagwati and Padma Desai, *India: Planning for Industrialization—Industrialization and Trade Policies since 1951* (London: Oxford University Press, 1970), pp. 231, 250.

7. Lok Sabha, Secretariat, *Ninth Report of the Committee on Industrial Licensing* (New Delhi, 1967), pp. 135–136.

8. Bhagwati and Desai, *India: Planning,* pp. 261–262, 304–305.

9. Ibid., p. 261.

10. Ibid., pp. 232, 241.

CHAPTER 7

1. See the conclusion to chapter 4.

2. Bert F. Hoselitz, *Sociological Aspects of Economic Growth* (New York: Free Press, 1960), pp. 154–156.

3. G. D. Berreman, "Caste in India and the United States," *American Journal of Sociology* 66 (1960):120–127.

4. Carroll, *Filipino Manufacturing Entrepreneur,* pp. 100, 126.

5. Calculated value of $\chi^2 = 193.51$, $\chi^2_{.01}$ with 1 d.f. $= 6.64$.

6. Calculated value of $\chi^2 = 7,394.72$, $\chi^2_{.01}$ with 1 d.f. $= 6.64$.

7. Orvis F. Collins, David G. Moore, and Darab B. Unwalla, *The Enterprising Man* (East Lansing, Mich.: MSU Business Studies, 1964), p. 238.

8. The observed frequency of fathers with less skilled work was 19, compared to an expected frequency (based on the general labor force) of 49. The observed frequency of fathers in business and professional work was 46, and the expected frequency, 21. Calculated value of $\chi^2 = 48.13$, $\chi^2_{.01}$ with 1 d.f. $= 6.64$.

9. Collins, Moore, and Unwalla, *The Enterprising Man,* p. 239.

10. W. Lloyd Warner and James C. Abegglen, *Occupational Mobility in American Business and Industry* (Minneapolis: University of Minnesota Press, 1955), pp. 41–42. These findings are reinforced by Mable Newcomer's figures on U.S. big business executives in *The Big Business Executive: The Factors That Made Him, 1900–1950* (New York: Columbia University Press, 1955), p. 55.

11. See Newcomer, *Big Business Executive,* p. 48; Warner and Abegglen, *Occupational Mobility,* pp. 239–249; G. William Domhoff, *Who Rules America* (Englewood Cliffs: Prentice-Hall, 1967), pp. 29–30.

12. David Granick, *The Red Executive: A Study of the Organization Man in Russian Industry* (New York: Anchor Books, 1961), pp. 39–40.

13. Harris, "Nigerian Entrepreneurship," p. 337; A. P. Alexander, *Greek Industrialists,* pp. 80–95; Collins, Moore, and Unwalla, *The Enterprising Man,* p. 238; Nafziger, *African Capitalism,* p. 180.

14. I did not ask the entrepreneurs questions concerning intergenerational upward mobility, since I considered the relationship found in the four studies

cited in note 13 generally well established. I would concede that if I had asked Vizag entrepreneurs questions of this type, my results would probably have supported the view that entrepreneurs were generally better off economically than their fathers.

15. Although Harris does classify the socioeconomic status of the entrepreneurs into highest, upper, middle, lower, and lowest, this information is used to correlate the status of the entrepreneurs and their fathers, and cannot be utilized to compare the socioeconomic class background of entrepreneurs to the general population. He indicates that a rough index—one that "is necessarily subjective"—was constructed on the basis of occupation, income, and positions of leadership within society. (Harris, "Industrial Entrepreneurship," pp. 256, 363.) Apparently the ranking of occupations is based on prestige ratings by Nigerian economics and medical students at the University of Ibadan, as reported by Robert W. Morgan, Jr., "Occupational Prestige Ratings by Nigerian Students," *Nigerian Journal of Economic and Social Studies* 7, no. 3 (November 1965):325-332; Harris, "Industrial Entrepreneurship," p. 363. It also appears that the socioeconomic status of fathers who were unskilled laborers was "lower" or "lowest" (categories which comprised 22.8 percent of the 254 fathers). This is not substantially inconsistent with the class rankings of these workers in Western countries, or with the assumptions of the respondents in my sample (see the discussion in chapter 4 on "Paternal Economic Status"). However it should be pointed out that the incomes of unskilled workers in the 1940s and 1950s in Nigeria were above average, since about four-fifths of the population was engaged in the low-income agricultural sector.

16. I am indebted to Eugene Staley for several suggestions for improving the discussion concerning the implications of the study for future research.

APPENDIX A

1. Each of the three largest firms had seventy-five or more employees, and the seven smallest firms had less than five employed. Some of the firms that were listed as having five or more employees at an earlier date, had cut employment to less than five by the time of interview. Table 6 gives more detail concerning the median employment of the firm.

2. Jan H. van der Veen, *A Study of Small Industries in Gujarat State, India,* Occasional Paper No. 65, Employment and Income Distribution Project, Department of Agricultural Economics (Ithaca: Cornell University, May 1973), p. 7.

3. Receiving relatively forthright information of income is not surprising when one understands both south Indian customs and the specific research context. The letter of introduction from a representative of a prestigious local university, the assurance of confidentiality in the letter, and the presence of a

visiting foreign researcher at the interview, usually alleviated the suspicions, at least by the last part of the interview, that there was some risk in providing information on receipts, expenses, net worth, and income. Perhaps as important is the fact that inquiries about income are not uncommon in the Indian context, even by virtual strangers. The visiting Western male soon learns that there is no taboo on the question, "How much money do you make?" but that to ask the question, "How is your wife?" is improper.

4. In seven of the firms, Telugu was used throughout the entire interview. In eleven additional instances, Telugu was used some of the time. The translation of concepts and questions into Telugu was carefully checked prior to their use.

APPENDIX C

1. K. J. Christopher, "Socio-Psychological Factors Influencing the Starting of a Small Industry Unit," *Indian Council of Social Science Research Abstracts,* 1970, p. 26.

2. Ibid., p. 22.

3. Ibid., p. 24.

BIBLIOGRAPHY

Aitken, Hugh G. H., ed. *Explorations in Enterprise*. Cambridge: Harvard University Press, 1965.

Alexander, Alec P. *Greek Industrialists: An Economic and Social Analysis*. Athens: Center of Planning and Economic Research, 1964.

_____. "Industrial Entrepreneurship in Turkey: Origins and Growth." *Economic Development and Cultural Change* 8, no. 4, pt. 1 (July 1960): 349–365.

Alexander, P. C. *Industrial Estates in India*. Bombay: Asia Publishing House, 1963.

Baran, Paul A. *The Political Economy of Growth*. New York: Monthly Review Press, 1957.

Baumol, William J. "Entrepreneurship in Economic Theory." *American Economic Review* 58, no. 2 (May 1968): 64–71.

Berna, James J. *Industrial Entrepreneurship in Madras State*. New York: Asia Publishing House, 1960.

Bhagwati, Jagdish N., and Desai, Padma. *India: Planning for Industrialization and Trade Policies since 1951*. London: Oxford University Press, 1970.

Brimmer, Andrew F. "The Setting of Entrepreneurship in India." *Quarterly Journal of Economics* 29, no. 4 (November 1955): 553–576.

Cantillon, Richard. *Essai sur la Nature Commerce en General*. Translated by Henry Higgs. London: Frank Cass and Co., 1959.

Carroll, John J. *The Filipino Manufacturing Entrepreneur, Agent and Product of Change*. Ithaca: Cornell University Press, 1965.

Christopher, K. J. "Socio-Psychological Factors Influencing the Starting of Small Industry Unit." *Indian Council of Social Science Research Abstracts* (1970), pp. 20-39.

Clemence, Richard V., and Doody, Francis S. *The Schumpeterian System.* Cambridge, Mass.: Addison-Wesley Press, Inc., 1950.

Cole, Arthur H. *Business Enterprise in its Social Setting.* Cambridge, Mass.: Harvard University Press, 1959.

Collins, Orvis F., Moore, David G., and Unwalla, Darab B. *The Enterprising Man.* East Lansing: MSU Business Studies, 1964.

Dobb, Maurice. *Capitalist Enterprise and Social Progress.* London: Routledge, 1926.

Epstein, T. S. *Economic Development and Social Change in South Asia.* Manchester: Manchester University Press, 1962.

Gadgil, Dhananjaya Ramchandra. *Origins of the Modern Indian Business Class—An Interim Report.* New York: Institute of Pacific Relations, 1959.

Gillion, Kenneth L. *Ahmadabad: A Study in Indian Urban History.* Berkeley: University of California Press, 1968.

Granick, David. *The Red Executive: A Study of the Organization Man in Russian Industry.* New York: Anchor Books, 1961.

Guha, Amalendu. "The Comprador Role of Parsi Seths, 1750-1850." *Economic and Political Weekly* 5 (28 November 1970): 1933-36.

_____. "Parsi Seths as Entrepreneurs, 1750-1850." *Economic and Political Weekly* 5 (29 August 1970): M. 107-M. 115.

Hagen, Everett E. *On the Theory of Social Change.* Homewood, Ill.: Dorsey Press, 1962.

Harbison, Frederick. "Entrepreneurial Organization as a Factor in Economic Development." *Quarterly Journal of Economics* 64, no. 3 (August 1956): 364-379.

Harris, John R. "Industrial Entrepreneurship in Nigeria." Ph.D. dissertation, Northwestern University, 1967.

_____. "Nigerian Entrepreneurship in Industry." *Entrepreneurship and Economic Development.* Edited by Peter Kilby. New York: The Free Press, 1971.

Hazari, R. K. *The Structure of the Corporate Private Sector: A Study of Concentration, Ownership and Control.* Bombay: Asia Publishing House, 1966.

Hazlehurst, Leighton W. *Entrepreneurship and the Merchant Castes in a Punjabi City.* Durham: Duke University Commonwealth Studies Center, 1966.

Hoselitz, Bert F. "Entrepreneurship and Traditional Elites." *Explorations in Entrepreneurial History/Second Series* 1 (Fall 1963): 36-49.

_____. *Sociological Aspects of Economic Growth.* New York: The Free Press, 1960.

Javillonar, Gloria V., and Peters, George R. "Sociological and Social Psychological Aspects of Indian Entrepreneurship." *British Journal of Sociology* 24, no. 3 (September 1973): 314–328.

Kilby, Peter. *African Enterprise: The Nigerian Bread Industry.* Stanford: Hoover Institution, 1965.

_____, ed. *Entrepreneurship and Economic Development.* New York: Free Press, 1971.

Kling, Blair B. "Obstacles to Entrepreneurship in India: The Case of Bengal." Paper presented to the Congress of Orientalists, University of Michigan, Ann Arbor, August 1967.

_____. "The Origins of the Managing Agency System in India." *Journal of Asian Studies* 26, no. 1 (November 1966): 37–47.

Knight, Frank. *Risk, Uncertainty and Profit.* Boston: Houghton Mifflin Co., 1921.

Koppel, Bruce, and Peterson, Richard E. "Industrial Entrepreneurship in India: A Reevaluation." *Developing Economies* 13, no. 3 (September 1975): 318–330.

Lamb, Helen B. "The Rise of Indian Business Communities." *Pacific Affairs* 23, no. 2 (June 1955): 101–116.

Leibenstein, Harvey. "Allocative Efficiency vs. 'X-Efficiency'." *American Economic Review* 56, no. 3 (June 1966): 392–415.

_____. "Entrepreneurship and Development." *American Economic Review* 58, no. 2 (May 1968): 72–83.

McClelland, David C. *The Achieving Society.* Princeton: D. Van Nostrand Company, 1961.

McClelland, David C., and Winter, David G. *Motivating Economic Achievement—Accelerating Economic Development Through Psychological Training.* New York: The Free Press, 1971.

McCrory, James T. *Case Studies in Latent Industrial Potential: Small Industry in a North Indian Town.* Delhi: Government of India, Ministry of Commerce and Industry, 1956.

Maclaurin, W. Robert. "The Sequence from Invention to Innovation and its Relation to Economic Growth." *Quarterly Journal of Economics* 67, no. 1 (February 1953): 97–111.

Marriott, McKim. *Caste Ranking and Community Structure in Five Regions of India and Pakistan.* Poona: Deccan College Postgraduate and Research Institute, 1965.

Marshall, Alfred. *Principles of Economics.* 1st ed. London: Macmillan, 1890.

Medhora, Phiroze B. "Entrepreneurship in India." *Political Science Quarterly* 80, no. 4 (September 1965): 562–578.

Morse, Richard. *Local Entrepreneurial Initiatives and Development in the Philippines, Malaysia, Indonesia and India Research Observations.* Unpublished report. East-West Technology and Development Institute, Honolulu, 18 February 1975.

Nafziger, E. Wayne. *African Capitalism: A Case Study in Nigerian Entrepreneurship.* Stanford: Hoover Institution, 1977.

——. "The Effect of the Nigerian Extended Family on Entrepreneurial Activity." *Economic Development and Cultural Change* 18, no. 1, pt. 1 (October 1969): 25–33.

——. "The Market for Nigerian Entrepreneurs." *South of the Sahara: Development in African Economies.* Edited by Sayre P. Schatz. London: Macmillan, 1972.

——. "The Mennonite Ethic in the Weberian Framework." *Explorations in Entrepreneurial History/Second Series* 2, no. 1 (Spring–Summer 1965): 187–204.

——. "The Relationship Between Education and Entrepreneurship in Nigeria." *The Journal of Developing Areas* 4 (April 1970): 349–360.

Newcomer, Mable. *The Big Business Executive: The Factors That Made Him, 1900–1950.* New York: Columbia University Press, 1955.

Owens, Raymond. "Peasant Entrepreneurs in an Industrial City." *Entrepreneurship and Modernization of Occupational Cultures in South Asia.* Edited by Milton Singer. Durham: Duke University Press, 1973.

Papanek, Gustav F. "The Development of Entrepreneurship." *American Economic Review* 52, no. 2 (May 1962): 46–58.

——. *Pakistan's Development: Social Goals and Private Incentives.* Cambridge: Harvard University Press, 1967.

Prasad, S. B., and Negandhi, A. R. *Managerialism for Economic Development: Essays on India.* The Hague: Martinus Nijhoff, 1968.

Ramana, Kanisetti Venkata. "Caste and Society in an Andhra Town." Ph.D. dissertation, University of Illinois, 1971.

Rao, N. A. "The Commerical Entrepreneurs in Visakhapatnam City: A Survey." Andhra University Department of Cooperation and Applied Economics, Waltair, 1971.

Rosen, Bernard C. "Race, Ethnicity and the Achievement Syndrome." *American Sociological Review* 24, no. 1 (February 1959): 47–60.

Rungta, Radhe Shyam. *The Rise of Business Corporations in India 1851–1900.* Cambridge: Cambridge University Press, 1970.

Say, J. B. *A Treatise on Political Economy.* Translated by C. R. Prinsap. 2 vols. 4th ed. Boston: Wells and Lilly, 1824.

Sayigh, Yusif A. *Entrepreneurs of Lebanon: The Role of the Business*

Leaders in a Developing Economy. Cambridge: Harvard University Press, 1962.

Schumpeter, Joseph A. *Business Cycles.* 2 vols. New York: McGraw-Hill Book Company, Inc., 1939.

_____. "Economic Theory and Entrepreneurial History." *Change and the Entrepreneur: Postulates and Patterns for Entrepreneurial History.* Harvard University Center in Entrepreneurial History. Cambridge, Mass.: Harvard University Press, 1949.

_____. *The Theory of Economic Development: An Inquiry into Profits, Capital, Credit, Interest, and the Business Cycle.* Translated by Redvers Opie. New York: Oxford University Press, 1961.

Sharma, R. A. "Emerging Patterns of Industrial Entrepreneurship in India." *Developing Economics* 11, no. 1 (March 1973): 39-61.

Singer, Milton. *When a Great Tradition Modernizes.* New York: Praeger Publications, 1972.

Singer, Milton, and Cohn, Bernard S., eds. *Structure and Change in Indian Society.* Chicago: Aldine Publishing Co., 1968.

Singh, Pritam. "Essays Concerning Some Types of Entrepreneurship in India." Ph.D. dissertation, University of Michigan, 1963.

Smith, Adam. *An Enquiry into the Nature and Causes of the Wealth of Nations.* 2 vols. London: G. Bell and Sons, 1912.

Soltow, James H. "The Entrepreneur in Economic History." *American Economic Review* 58, no. 2 (May 1968): 84-92.

Spodek, Howard. "The Manchesterisation of Ahmadabad." *Economic Weekly* 17 (13 March 1965): 483-490.

_____. "Traditional Culture and Entrepreneurship: A Case Study of Ahmadabad." *Economic and Political Weekly* 4 (22 February 1969): M. 27-M. 31.

Srinivas, M. N. *Caste in Modern India and Other Essays.* New York: Asia Publishing House, 1962.

Timberg, Thomas A. *Industrial Entrepreneurship Among the Trading Communities of India: How the Pattern Differs.* Center for International Affairs, Development Advisory Service, Economic Development Report No. 136, Harvard University, July 1969.

Tyagarajan, Meenakshi. "The Development of the Theory of Entrepreneurship." *Indian Economic Review* 4, no. 4 (August 1959): 135-150.

Van der Veen, Jan H. *A Study of Small Industries in Gujarat State, India.* Occasional Paper No. 65, Employment and Income Distribution Project, Department of Agricultural Economics, Ithaca, Cornell University, May 1973.

Walras, Leon. *Elements of Pure Economics or the Theory of Social Wealth.* London: George Allen and Unwin, 1954.

Warner, W. Lloyd, and Abegglen, James C. *Occupational Mobility in American Business and Industry*. Minneapolis: University of Minnesota Press, 1955.

Weber, Max. *The Protestant Ethic and the Spirit of Capitalism*. Translated by Talcott Parsons. New York: Charles Scribner's Sons, 1958.

―――. *The Religion of India—The Sociology of Hinduism and Buddhism*. New York: The Free Press, 1958.

INDEX

ꭹ Production Notes

This book was designed by Roger J. Eggers and typeset on the Unified Composing System by the design and production staff of The University Press of Hawaii.

The text typeface is English Times and the display typeface is Friz Quadrata.

Offset presswork and binding were done by Halliday Lithograph. Text paper is Glatfelter P & S Offset, basis 55.